# Esperanza Rising

## with Connections

# Esperanza Rising

Pam Muñoz Ryan

with
Connections

**HOLT, RINEHART AND WINSTON**

A Harcourt Classroom Education Company

Austin · New York · Orlando · Atlanta · San Francisco · Boston · Dallas · Toronto · London

Requests for permission to make copies of any part of the work should be mailed to the following address: Permissions Department, Holt, Rinehart and Winston, 10801 N. MoPac Expressway, Building 3, Austin, Texas 78759.

For permission to reprint copyrighted material, grateful acknowledgment is made to the following sources:

**Scholastic Inc.:** *Esperanza Rising* by Pam Muñoz Ryan. Copyright © 2000 by Pam Muñoz Ryan.

**Dell Publishing, a division of Random House, Inc.:** "The Winter Hibiscus" by Minfong Ho from *Join In: Multiethnic Short Stories,* edited by Donald R. Gallo. Copyright © 1993 by Minfong Ho. **HarperCollins Publishers:** "Crossing the Creek" from *Little House on the Prairie* by Laura Ingalls Wilder. Copyright 1935 by Laura Ingalls Wilder. **Los Angeles Times:** From "5 Part Series on Cesar Chavez" by Gloria Miklowitz from *Los Angeles Times,* October 3–6, 2000. Copyright © 2000 by Los Angeles Times. **Merlyn's Pen, Inc.:** "A List of 10 Things" by Loubel Cruz from *Short Takes: Brief Personal Narratives and Other Works by American Teen Writers,* edited by Kathryn Kulpa. Copyright © 1995 by Merlyn's Pen, Inc. **Museum Steps Music:** Lyrics from "Ellis Island" by Marc Cohn from *Burning the Daze.* Copyright © 1998 by Museum Steps Music. All rights reserved.

Cover: background, Stone/David Barnes; oranges, Image Copyright © 2001 PhotoDisc, Inc./HRW; Esperanza, Victoria Smith/HRW Photo.

ISBN 0-03-066351-2

9  10  043  08  07  06

# Contents

1924

"Our land is alive, Esperanza," said Papa, taking her small hand as they walked through the gentle slopes of the vineyard. Leafy green vines draped the arbors and the grapes were ready to drop. Esperanza was six years old and loved to walk with her papa through the winding rows, gazing up at him and watching his eyes dance with love for the land.

"This whole valley breathes and lives," he said, sweeping his arm toward the distant mountains that guarded them. "It gives us the grapes and then they welcome us." He gently touched a wild tendril that reached into the row, as if it had been waiting to shake his hand. He picked up a handful of earth and studied it. "Did you know that when you lie down on the land, you can feel it breathe? That you can feel its heart beating?"

"Papi, I want to feel it," she said.

"Come." They walked to the end of the row,

1

where the incline of the land formed a grassy swell.

Papa lay down on his stomach and looked up at her, patting the ground next to him.

Esperanza smoothed her dress and knelt down. Then, like a caterpillar, she slowly inched flat next to him, their faces looking at each other. The warm sun pressed on one of Esperanza's cheeks and the warm earth on the other.

She giggled.

"Shhh," he said. "You can only feel the earth's heartbeat when you are still and quiet."

She swallowed her laughter and after a moment said, "I can't hear it, Papi."

"*Aguántate tantito y la fruta caerá en tu mano*," he said. "Wait a little while and the fruit will fall into your hand. You must be patient, Esperanza."

She waited and lay silent, watching Papa's eyes.

And then she felt it. Softly at first. A gentle thumping. Then stronger. A resounding thud, thud, thud against her body.

She could hear it, too. The beat rushing in her ears. *Shoomp, shoomp, shoomp.*

She stared at Papa, not wanting to say a word. Not wanting to lose the sound. Not wanting to forget the feel of the heart of the valley.

She pressed closer to the ground, until her body was breathing with the earth's. And with Papa's. The three hearts beating together.

She smiled at Papa, not needing to talk, her eyes saying everything.

And his smile answered hers. Telling her that he knew she had felt it.

# LAS UVAS
GRAPES

## six years later

Papa handed Esperanza the knife. The short blade was curved like a scythe, its fat wooden handle fitting snugly in her palm. This job was usually reserved for the eldest son of a wealthy rancher, but since Esperanza was an only child and Papa's pride and glory, she was always given the honor. Last night she had watched Papa sharpen the knife back and forth across a stone, so she knew the tool was edged like a razor.

"*Cuídate los dedos*," said Papa. "Watch your fingers."

The August sun promised a dry afternoon in Aguascalientes, Mexico. Everyone who lived and worked on El Rancho de las Rosas was gathered at the edge of the field: Esperanza's family, the house servants in their long white aprons, the *vaqueros* already sitting on their horses ready to ride out to the cattle, and fifty or sixty *campesinos*, straw hats in their hands, holding their own knives ready. They were covered top to bottom, in long-sleeved shirts, baggy pants tied at the ankles with string, and bandanas wrapped around their foreheads and necks to protect them from the sun, dust, and spiders. Esperanza, on the other hand, wore a light silk dress that stopped above her summer boots, and no hat. On top of her head a wide satin ribbon was tied in a big bow, the tails trailing in her long black hair.

The clusters were heavy on the vine and ready to deliver. Esperanza's parents, Ramona and Sixto Ortega, stood nearby, Mama, tall and elegant, her hair in the usual braided wreath that crowned her head, and Papa, barely taller than Mama, his graying mustache twisted up at the sides. He swept his hand toward the grapevines, signaling Esperanza. When she walked toward the arbors and glanced back at her parents, they both smiled and nodded, encouraging her forward. When she reached the vines, she separated the leaves and carefully grasped a thick stem. She put the knife to it, and with a quick swipe, the heavy cluster of grapes dropped into her waiting hand. Esperanza walked back to Papa and handed him the fruit. Papa kissed it and held it up for all to see.

"*¡La cosecha!*" said Papa. "Harvest!"

"*¡Ole! ¡Ole!*" A cheer echoed around them.

The *campesinos,* the field-workers, spread out over the land and began the task of reaping the fields. Esperanza stood between Mama and Papa, with her arms linked to theirs, and admired the activity of the workers.

"Papi, this is my favorite time of year," she said, watching the brightly colored shirts of the workers slowly moving among the arbors. Wagons rattled back and forth from the fields to the big barns where the grapes would be stored until they went to the winery.

"Is the reason because when the picking is done, it will be someone's birthday and time for a big *fiesta?*" Papa asked.

Esperanza smiled. When the grapes delivered their harvest, she always turned another year. This year, she would be thirteen. The picking would take three weeks and then, like every other year, Mama and Papa would host a *fiesta* for the harvest. And for her birthday.

Marisol Rodríguez, her best friend, would come with her family to celebrate. Her father was a fruit rancher and they lived on the neighboring property. Even though their houses were acres apart, they met every Saturday beneath the holm oak on a rise between the two ranches. Her other friends, Chita and Bertina, would be at the party, too, but they lived farther away and Esperanza didn't see them as often. Their classes at St. Francis didn't start again until after the harvest and she couldn't wait to see them. When they were all together, they talked about one thing: their *Quinceañeras*, the presentation parties they would have when they turned fifteen. They still had two more years to wait, but so much to discuss — the beautiful white gowns they would wear, the big celebrations where they would be presented, and the sons of the richest families who would dance with them. After their *Quinceañeras*, they would be old enough to be courted, marry, and become *las patronas*, the heads of their households, rising to the positions of their mothers before them. Esperanza preferred to think, though, that she and her someday-husband would live with Mama and Papa forever. Because she couldn't imagine living anywhere other than El Rancho de las Rosas. Or with any fewer servants. Or without being surrounded by the people who adored her.

It had taken every day of three weeks to put the harvest to bed and now everyone anticipated the celebration. Esperanza remembered Mama's instructions as she gathered roses from Papa's garden.

"Tomorrow, bouquets of roses and baskets of grapes on every table."

Papa had promised to meet her in the garden and he never disappointed her. She bent over to pick a red bloom, fully opened, and pricked her finger on a vicious thorn. Big pearls of blood pulsed from the tip of her thumb and she automatically thought, "bad luck." She quickly wrapped her hand in the corner of her apron and dismissed the premonition. Then she cautiously clipped the blown rose that had wounded her. Looking toward the horizon, she saw the last of the sun disappear behind the Sierra Madre. Darkness would settle quickly and a feeling of uneasiness and worry nagged at her.

Where was Papa? He had left early that morning with the *vaqueros* to work the cattle. And he was always home before sundown, dusty from the mesquite grasslands and stamping his feet on the patio to get rid of the crusty dirt on his boots. Sometimes he even brought beef jerky that the cattlemen had made, but Esperanza always had to find it first, searching his shirt pockets while he hugged her.

Tomorrow was her birthday and she knew that she would be serenaded at sunrise. Papa and the men who lived on the ranch would congregate below her window, their rich, sweet voices singing *Las Mañanitas*, the birthday song. She would run to her window and wave kisses to Papa and the others, then downstairs she would open her gifts. She knew there would be a porcelain doll from

Papa. He had given her one every year since she was born. And Mama would give her something she had made: linens, camisoles or blouses embroidered with her beautiful needlework. The linens always went into the trunk at the end of her bed for *algún día*, for someday.

Esperanza's thumb would not stop bleeding. She picked up the basket of roses and hurried from the garden, stopping on the patio to rinse her hand in the stone fountain. As the water soothed her, she looked through the massive wooden gates that opened onto thousands of acres of Papa's land.

Esperanza strained her eyes to see a dust cloud that meant riders were near and that Papa was finally home. But she saw nothing. In the dusky light, she walked around the courtyard to the back of the large adobe and wood house. There she found Mama searching the horizon, too.

"Mama, my finger. An angry thorn stabbed me," said Esperanza.

"Bad luck," said Mama, confirming the superstition, but she half-smiled. They both knew that bad luck could mean nothing more than dropping a pan of water or breaking an egg.

Mama put her arms around Esperanza's waist and both sets of eyes swept over the corrals, stables, and servants' quarters that sprawled in the distance. Esperanza was almost as tall as Mama and everyone said she would someday look just like her beautiful mother. Sometimes, when Esperanza twisted her hair on top of her head and looked in the mirror, she could see that it was almost true. There was the same black hair, wavy and thick. Same dark lashes and fair, creamy skin. But it wasn't precisely Mama's face, because Papa's eyes were there too, shaped like fat, brown almonds.

"He is just a little late," said Mama. And part of Esperanza's mind believed her. But the other part scolded him.

"Mama, the neighbors warned him just last night about bandits."

Mama nodded and bit the corner of her lip in worry. They both knew that even though it was

1930 and the revolution in Mexico had been over for ten years, there was still resentment against the large landowners.

"Change has not come fast enough, Esperanza. The wealthy still own most of the land while some of the poor have not even a garden plot. There are cattle grazing on the big ranches yet some peasants are forced to eat cats. Papa is sympathetic and has given land to many of his workers. The people know that."

"But Mama, do the bandits know that?"

"I hope so," said Mama quietly. "I have already sent Alfonso and Miguel to look for him. Let's wait inside."

~

Tea was ready in Papa's study and so was Abuelita.

"Come, *mi nieta*, my granddaughter," said Abuelita, holding up yarn and crochet hooks. "I am starting a new blanket and will teach you the zigzag."

Esperanza's grandmother, whom everyone

called Abuelita, lived with them and was a smaller, older, more wrinkled version of Mama. She looked very distinguished, wearing a respectable black dress, the same gold loops she wore in her ears every day, and her white hair pulled back into a bun at the nape of her neck. But Esperanza loved her more for her capricious ways than for her propriety. Abuelita might host a group of ladies for a formal tea in the afternoon, then after they had gone, be found wandering barefoot in the grapes, with a book in her hand, quoting poetry to the birds. Although some things were always the same with Abuelita — a lace-edged handkerchief peeking out from beneath the sleeve of her dress — others were surprising: a flower in her hair, a beautiful stone in her pocket, or a philosophical saying salted into her conversation. When Abuelita walked into a room, everyone scrambled to make her comfortable. Even Papa would give up his chair for her.

Esperanza complained, "Must we always crochet to take our minds off worry?" She sat next to her grandmother anyway, smelling her ever-present aroma of garlic, face powder, and peppermint.

"What happened to your finger?" asked Abuelita.

"A big thorn," said Esperanza.

Abuelita nodded and said thoughtfully, "*No hay rosa sin espinas.* There is no rose without thorns."

Esperanza smiled, knowing that Abuelita wasn't talking about flowers at all but that there was no life without difficulties. She watched the silver crochet needle dance back and forth in her grandmother's hand. When a strand of hair fell into her lap, Abuelita picked it up and held it against the yarn and stitched it into the blanket.

"Esperanza, in this way my love and good wishes will be in the blanket forever. Now watch. Ten stitches up to the top of the mountain. Add one stitch. Nine stitches down to the bottom of the valley. Skip one."

Esperanza picked up her own crochet needle and copied Abuelita's movements and then looked at her own crocheting. The tops of her mountains were lopsided and the bottoms of her valleys were all bunched up.

Abuelita smiled, reached over, and pulled the yarn, unraveling all of Esperanza's rows. "Do not be afraid to start over," she said.

Esperanza sighed and began again with ten stitches.

Softly humming, Hortensia, the housekeeper, came in with a plate of small sandwiches. She offered one to Mama.

"No, thank you," said Mama.

Hortensia set the tray down and brought a shawl and wrapped it protectively around Mama's shoulders. Esperanza couldn't remember a time when Hortensia had not taken care of them. She was a Zapotec Indian from Oaxaca, with a short, solid figure and blue-black hair in a braid down her back. Esperanza watched the two women look out into the dark and couldn't help but think that Hortensia was almost the opposite of Mama.

"Don't worry so much," said Hortensia. "Alfonso and Miguel will find him."

Alfonso, Hortensia's husband, was *el jefe*, the boss, of all the field-workers and Papa's *compañero*, his close friend and companion. He had the same dark skin and small stature as Hortensia, and Esperanza thought his round eyes, long eyelids, and droopy mustache made him look like a forlorn puppy. He was anything but sad, though. He loved the land as Papa did and it had been the two of them, working side by side, who had resurrected the neglected rose garden that had been in the family for generations. Alfonso's brother worked in the United States so Alfonso always talked about going there someday, but he stayed in Mexico because of his attachment to Papa and El Rancho de las Rosas.

Miguel was Alfonso and Hortensia's son, and he and Esperanza had played together since they were babies. At sixteen, he was already taller than both of his parents. He had their dark skin and Alfonso's big, sleepy eyes, and thick eyebrows that Esperanza always thought would grow into one. It was true that he knew the farthest reaches of the ranch better than anyone. Since Miguel was a young boy, Papa had taken him to parts of the property that even Esperanza and Mama had never seen.

When she was younger, Esperanza used to complain, "Why does he always get to go and not me?"

Papa would say, "Because he knows how to fix things and he is learning his job."

Miguel would look at her and before riding off with Papa, he would give her a taunting smile. But what Papa said was true, too. Miguel had patience and quiet strength and could figure out how to fix anything: plows and tractors, especially anything with a motor.

Several years ago, when Esperanza was still a young girl, Mama and Papa had been discussing boys from "good families" whom Esperanza should meet someday. She couldn't imagine being matched with someone she had never met. So she announced, "I am going to marry Miguel!"

Mama had laughed at her and said, "You will feel differently as you get older."

"No, I won't," Esperanza had said stubbornly.

But now that she was a young woman, she understood that Miguel was the housekeeper's son and she was the ranch owner's daughter and between them ran a deep river. Esperanza stood on one side and Miguel stood on the other and the river could never be crossed. In a moment of self-importance, Esperanza had told all of this to Miguel. Since then, he had spoken only a few words to her. When their paths crossed, he nodded and said politely, "*Mi reina*, my queen," but nothing more. There was no teasing or laughing or talking about every little thing. Esperanza pretended not to care, though she secretly wished she had never told Miguel about the river.

Distracted, Mama paced at the window, each step making a hollow tapping sound on the tile floor.

Hortensia lit the lamps.

The minutes passed into hours.

"I hear riders," said Mama, and she ran for the door.

But it was only Tío Luis and Tío Marco, Papa's

older stepbrothers. Tío Luis was the bank president and Tío Marco was the mayor of the town. Esperanza didn't care how important they were because she did not like them. They were serious and gloomy and always held their chins too high. Tío Luis was the eldest and Tío Marco, who was a few years younger and not as smart, always followed his older brother's lead, like *un burro*, a donkey. Even though Tío Marco was the mayor, he did everything Tío Luis told him to do. They were both tall and skinny, with tiny mustaches and white beards on just the tips of their chins. Esperanza could tell that Mama didn't like them either, but she was always polite because they were Papa's family. Mama had even hosted parties for Tío Marco when he ran for mayor. Neither had ever married and Papa said it was because they loved money and power more than people. Esperanza thought it was because they looked like two underfed billy goats.

"Ramona," said Tío Luis. "We may have bad news. One of the *vaqueros* brought this to us."

He handed Mama Papa's silver belt buckle, the only one of its kind, engraved with the brand of the ranch.

Mama's face whitened. She examined it, turning it over and over in her hand. "It may mean nothing," she said. Then, ignoring them, she turned toward the window and began pacing again, still clutching the belt buckle.

"We will wait with you in your time of need," said Tío Luis, and as he passed Esperanza, he patted her shoulder and gave it a gentle squeeze.

Esperanza stared after him. In her entire life, she couldn't remember him ever touching her. Her uncles were not like those of her friends. They never spoke to her, played or even teased her. In fact, they acted as if she didn't exist at all. And for that reason, Tío Luis's sudden kindness made her shiver with fear for Papa.

Abuelita and Hortensia began lighting candles and saying prayers for the men's safe return. Mama, with her arms hugging her chest, swayed back and forth at the window, never taking her eyes from the darkness. They tried to pass the time with small talk but their words dwindled into silence. Every sound of the house seemed magnified, the clock ticking, someone coughing, the clink of a teacup.

Esperanza struggled with her stitches. She tried to think about the *fiesta* and all the presents she would receive tomorrow. She tried to think of bouquets of roses and baskets of grapes on every table. She tried to think of Marisol and the other girls, giggling and telling stories. But those thoughts would only stay in her mind for a moment before transforming into worry, because she couldn't ignore the throbbing soreness in her thumb where the thorn had left its unlucky mark.

It wasn't until the candelabra held nothing but short stubs of tallow that Mama finally said, "I see a lantern. Someone is coming!"

They hurried to the courtyard and watched a distant light, a small beacon of hope swaying in the darkness.

The wagon came into view. Alfonso held the

reins and Miguel the lantern. When the wagon stopped, Esperanza could see a body in back, completely covered with a blanket.

"Where's Papa?" she cried.

Miguel hung his head. Alfonso didn't say a word but the tears running down his round cheeks confirmed the worst.

Mama fainted.

Abuelita and Hortensia ran to her side.

Esperanza felt her heart drop. A noise came from her mouth and slowly, her first breath of grief grew into a tormented cry. She fell to her knees and sank into a dark hole of despair and disbelief.

# LAS PAPAYAS

PAPAYAS

*"Estas son las mañanitas que cantaba el Rey David*

*a las muchachas bonitas; se las cantamos aquí.*

These are the morning songs which King David used to sing

to all the pretty girls; we sing them here to you."

Esperanza heard Papa and the others singing. They were outside her window and their voices were clear and melodic. Before she was aware, she smiled because her first thought was that today was her birthday. *I should get up and wave kisses to Papa.* But when she opened her eyes, she realized she was in her parents' bed, on Papa's side that still smelled like him, and the song had been in her dreams. Why hadn't she slept in her own room? Then the events of last night wrenched her mind into reality. Her smile faded, her chest tightened, and a heavy blanket of anguish smothered her smallest joy.

Papa and his *vaqueros* had been ambushed and killed while mending a fence on the farthest reaches of the ranch. The bandits stole their boots, saddles, and horses. And they even took the beef jerky that Papa had hidden in his pockets for Esperanza.

Esperanza got out of bed and wrapped *un chal* around her shoulders. The shawl felt heavier than usual. Was it the yarn? Or was her heart weighing her down? She went downstairs and stood in *la sala*, the large entry hall. The house was empty and silent. Where was everyone? Then she remembered that Abuelita and Alfonso were taking Mama to see the priest this morning. Before she could call for Hortensia, there was a knocking at the front door.

"Who is there?" called Esperanza through the door.

"It is Señor Rodríguez. I have the papayas."

Esperanza opened the door. Marisol's father stood before her, his hat in his hand. Beside him was a big box of papayas.

"Your father ordered these from me for the *fiesta*

today. I tried to deliver them to the kitchen but no one answered."

She stared at the man who had known Papa since he was a boy. Then she looked at the green papayas ripening to yellow. She knew why Papa had ordered them. Papaya, coconut, and lime salad was Esperanza's favorite and Hortensia made it every year on her birthday.

Her face crumbled. "Señor," she said, choking back tears. "Have you not heard? My . . . my papa is dead."

Señor Rodríguez stared blankly, then said, "¿Qué pasó, niña? What happened?"

She took a quivery breath. As she told the story, she watched the grief twist Señor Rodríguez's face and overtake him as he sat down on the patio bench, shaking his head. She felt as if she were in someone else's body, watching a sad scene but unable to help.

Hortensia walked out and put her arm around Esperanza. She nodded to Señor Rodríguez, then guided Esperanza back up the stairs to the bedroom.

"He ordered the pa . . . papayas," sobbed Esperanza.

"I know," whispered Hortensia, sitting next to her on the bed and rocking her back and forth. "I know."

⁓

The rosaries, masses, and funeral lasted three days. People whom Esperanza had never seen before came to the ranch to pay their respects. They brought enough food to feed ten families every day, and so many flowers that the overwhelming fragrance gave them all headaches and Hortensia finally put the bouquets outside.

Marisol came with Señor and Señora Rodríguez several times. In front of the adults, Esperanza modeled Mama's refined manners, accepting Marisol's condolences. But as soon as they could, the two girls excused themselves and went to Esperanza's room where they sat on her bed, held hands, and wept as one.

The house was full of visitors and their polite murmurings during the day. Mama was cordial and attentive to everyone, as if entertaining them gave her a purpose. At night, though, the house emptied. The rooms seemed too big without Papa's voice to fill them, and the echoes of their footsteps deepened their sadness. Abuelita sat by Mama's bed every night and stroked her head until she slept; then she would come around to the other side and do the same for Esperanza. But soon after, Esperanza often woke to Mama's soft crying. Or Mama woke to hers. And then they held each other, without letting go, until morning.

Esperanza avoided opening her birthday gifts. Every time she looked at the packages, they reminded her of the happy *fiesta* she was supposed to have. One morning, Mama finally insisted, saying, "Papa would have wanted it."

Abuelita handed Esperanza each gift and Esperanza methodically opened them and laid them back on the table. A white purse for Sundays, with a rosary inside from Marisol. A rope of blue beads from Chita. The book, *Don Quijote*, from Abuelita. A beautiful embroidered dresser scarf from Mama, for someday. Finally, she opened the box she knew was the doll. She couldn't help thinking that it was the last thing Papa would ever give her.

Hands trembling, she lifted the lid and looked inside the box. The doll wore a fine white batiste dress and a white lace *mantilla* over her black hair. Her porcelain face looked wistfully at Esperanza with enormous eyes.

"Oh, she looks like an angel," said Abuelita, taking her handkerchief from her sleeve and blotting her eyes. Mama said nothing but reached out and touched the doll's face.

Esperanza couldn't talk. Her heart felt so big and hurt so much that it crowded out her voice. She hugged the doll to her chest and walked out of the room, leaving all the other gifts behind.

~

Tío Luis and Tío Marco came every day and went into Papa's study to "take care of the family business." At first, they stayed only a few hours, but soon they became like *la calabaza*, the squash plant in Alfonso's garden, whose giant leaves spread out, encroaching upon anything smaller. The uncles eventually stayed each day until dark, taking all their meals at the ranch as well. Esperanza could tell that Mama was uneasy with their constant presence.

Finally, the lawyer came to settle the estate. Mama, Esperanza, and Abuelita sat properly in their black dresses as the uncles walked into the study.

A little too loudly, Tío Luis said, "Ramona, grieving does not suit you. I hope you will not wear black all year!"

Mama did not answer but maintained her composure.

They nodded to Abuelita but, as usual, said nothing to Esperanza.

The talk began about bank loans and investments. It all seemed so complicated to Esperanza and her mind wandered. She had not been in this room since Papa died. She looked around at Papa's desk and books, Mama's basket of crocheting with the silver crochet hooks that Papa had bought her in Guadalajara, the table near the door that held Papa's rose clippers and beyond the double doors, his garden. Her uncles' papers were strewn across the desk. Papa never kept his desk that way. Tío Luis sat in Papa's chair as if it were his own. And then Esperanza noticed the belt buckle. Papa's belt buckle on Tío Luis's belt. It was wrong. Everything was wrong. Tío Luis should not be sitting in Papa's chair. He should not be wearing Papa's belt buckle with the brand of the ranch on it! For the thousandth time, she wiped the tears that slipped down her face, but this time they were angry tears. A look of indignation passed between Mama and Abuelita. Were they feeling the same?

"Ramona," said the lawyer. "Your husband, Sixto Ortega, left this house and all of its contents to you and your daughter. You will also receive the yearly income from the grapes. As you know, it is not customary to leave land to women and since Luis was the banker on the loan, Sixto left the land to him."

"Which makes things rather awkward," said Tío Luis. "I am the bank president and would like to live accordingly. Now that I own this beautiful land, I would like to purchase the house from you for this amount." He handed Mama a piece of paper.

Mama looked at it and said, "This is our home. My husband meant for us to live here. And the house . . . it is worth twenty times this much! So no, I will not sell. Besides, where would we live?"

"I predicted you would say no, Ramona," said Tío Luis. "And I have a solution to your living arrangements. A proposal actually. One of marriage."

Who is he talking about? thought Esperanza. Who would marry him?

He cleared his throat. "Of course, we would wait the appropriate amount of time out of respect for my brother. One year is customary, is it not? Even you can see that with your beauty and reputation and my position at the bank, we could be a very powerful couple. Did you know that I, too, have been thinking of entering politics? I am going to campaign for governor. And what woman would not want to be the governor's wife?"

Esperanza could not believe what she heard. Mama marry Tío Luis? Marry a goat? She looked wide-eyed at him, then at Mama.

Mama's face looked as if it were in terrible pain. She stood up and spoke slowly and deliberately. "I have no desire to marry you, Luis, now or ever. Frankly, your offer offends me."

Tío Luis's face hardened like a rock and the muscles twitched in his narrow neck.

"You will regret your decision, Ramona. You must keep in mind that this house and those grapes are on my property. I can make things difficult for you. Very difficult. I will let you sleep on the decision, for it is more than generous."

Tío Luis and Tío Marco put on their hats and left.

The lawyer looked uncomfortable and began gathering documents.

"Vultures!" said Abuelita.

"Can he do this?" asked Mama.

"Yes," said the lawyer. "Technically, he is now your landlord."

"But he could build another house, bigger and more pretentious anywhere on the property," said Mama.

"It is not the house that he wants," said Abuelita. "It is your influence he wants. People in this territory loved Sixto and respect you. With you as his wife, Luis could win any election."

Mama stiffened. She looked at the lawyer and said, "Please officially relay this message to Luis. I will never, ever, change my mind."

"I will do that, Ramona," said the lawyer. "But be careful. He is a devious, dangerous man."

The lawyer left and Mama collapsed into a chair, put her head in her hands and began to cry.

Esperanza ran to her. "Don't cry, Mama. Everything will be all right." But she didn't sound convincing, even to herself. Because all she could think about was what Tío Luis had said, that Mama would regret her decision.

That evening, Hortensia and Alfonso sat with Mama and Abuelita discussing the problem. Esperanza paced and Miguel quietly looked on.

"Will the income from the grapes be enough to support the house and the servants?" said Mama.

"Maybe," said Alfonso.

"Then I will stay in my home," said Mama.

"Do you have any other money?" asked Alfonso.

"I have money in the bank," announced Abuelita. And then more quietly she added, "Luis's bank."

"He would prevent you from taking it out," said Hortensia.

"If we need help, we could borrow money from our friends. From Señor Rodríguez," said Esperanza.

"Your uncles are very powerful and corrupt," said Alfonso. "They can make things difficult for anyone who tries to help you. Remember, they are the banker and the mayor."

The conversation continued to go in circles. Esperanza finally excused herself. She walked out to Papa's garden and sat on a stone bench. Many of the roses had dropped their petals, leaving the stem and the rosehip, the green, grapelike fruit of the rose. Abuelita said the rosehip contained the memories of the roses and that when you drank tea made from it, you took in all the beauty that the plant had known. These roses have known Papa, she thought. She would ask Hortensia to make rosehip tea tomorrow.

Miguel found her in the garden and sat beside her. Since Papa died, he had been polite but still had not talked to her.

"Anza," he said, using her childhood name. "Which rose is yours?" In recent years, his voice had become a deep throttle. She hadn't realized how much she missed hearing it. The sound brought tears to her eyes but she quickly blinked them away. She pointed to the miniature pink blooms with delicate stems that climbed up the trellises.

"And where is mine?" asked Miguel, nudging her like he did when they were younger and told each other everything.

Esperanza smiled and pointed to the orange sunburst next to it. They had been young children the day Papa had planted one for each of them.

"What does it all mean, Miguel?"

"There are rumors in town that Luis intends to take over the ranch, one way or another. Now that it seems true, we will probably leave for the United States to work."

Esperanza shook her head as if to say no. She could not imagine living without Hortensia, Alfonso, and Miguel.

"My father and I have lost faith in our country. We were born servants here and no matter how hard we work we will always be servants. Your father was a good man. He gave us a small piece of land and a cabin. But your uncles . . . you know their reputation. They would take it all away and treat us like animals. We will not work for them. The work is hard in the United States but at least there we have a chance to be more than servants."

"But Mama and Abuelita . . . they need . . . we need you."

"My father says we won't leave until it is necessary." He reached over and took her hand. "I'm sorry about your papa."

His touch was warm and Esperanza's heart

skipped. She looked at her hand in his and felt the color rushing to her face. Surprised at her own blush, she pulled away from him. She stood and stared at the roses.

An awkward silence built a wall between them.

She glanced quickly at him.

He was still looking at her, with eyes full of hurt. Before Miguel left her there, he said softly, "You were right, Esperanza. In Mexico we stand on different sides of the river."

Esperanza went up to her room, thinking that nothing seemed right. She walked slowly around her bed, running her hand over the finely carved posts. She counted the dolls lined up on her dresser: thirteen, one for each birthday. When Papa was alive, everything was in order, like the dolls lined up in a row.

She put on a long cotton nightgown with hand-sewn lace, picked up the new doll and walked to the open window. Looking out over the valley, she wondered where they would go if they had to live somewhere else. They had no other family except Abuelita's sisters and they were nuns in a convent. "I won't ever leave here," she whispered.

A sudden breeze carried a familiar, pungent smell. She looked down into the courtyard and saw the wooden box still sitting on the patio. It held the papayas from Señor Rodríguez, the ones that Papa had ordered, that should have been served on her birthday. Their overripe sweetness now pervaded the air with each breath of wind.

She crawled into bed beneath the linens edged with lace. Hugging the doll, she tried to sleep but her thoughts kept returning to Tío Luis. She felt sick at the thought of Mama marrying him. Of course she had told him no! She took a deep breath, still smelling the papayas and Papa's sweet intentions.

*Why did Papa have to die? Why did he leave me and Mama?*

She closed her eyes tight and did what she tried to do each night. She tried to find the dream, the one where Papa was singing the birthday song.

# LOS HIGOS
### FIGS

The wind blew hard that night and the house moaned and whistled. Instead of dreaming of birthday songs, Esperanza's sleep was filled with nightmares. An enormous bear was chasing her, getting closer and closer and finally folding her in a tight embrace. Its fur caught in her mouth, making it hard to breathe. Someone tried to pull the bear away but couldn't. The bear squeezed harder until it was smothering Esperanza. Then when she thought she would suffocate, the bear grabbed her by the shoulders and shook her until her head wagged back and forth.

Her eyes opened, then closed again. She realized she was dreaming and for an instant, she felt relieved. But the shaking began again, harder this time.

Someone was calling her.

"Esperanza!"

She opened her eyes.

"Esperanza! Wake up!" screamed Mama. "The house is on fire!"

Smoke drifted into the room.

"Mama, what's happening?"

"Get up, Esperanza! We must get Abuelita!"

Esperanza heard Alfonso's deep voice yelling from somewhere downstairs.

"Señora Ortega! Esperanza!"

"Here! We are here!" called Mama, grabbing a damp rag from the washbowl and handing it to Esperanza to put over her mouth and nose. Esperanza swung around in a circle looking for something, anything, to save. She grabbed the doll. Then she and Mama hurried down the hall toward Abuelita's room, but it was empty.

"Alfonso!" screamed Mama. "Abuelita is not here!"

"We will find her. You must come now. The stairs are beginning to burn. Hurry!"

Esperanza held the towel over her face and looked down the stairs. Curtains flamed up the walls. The house was enveloped in a fog that

40

thickened toward the ceiling. Mama and Esperanza crouched down the stairs where Alfonso was waiting to lead them out through the kitchen.

In the courtyard, the wooden gates were open. Near the stables, the *vaqueros* were releasing the horses from the corrals. Servants scurried everywhere. Where were they going?

"Where's Abuelita? Abuelita!" cried Mama.

Esperanza felt dizzy. Nothing seemed real. Was she still dreaming? Was this her own imagination gone wild?

Miguel grabbed her. "Where's your mother and Abuelita?"

Esperanza whimpered and looked toward Mama. He left her, stopped at Mama, then ran toward the house.

The wind caught the sparks from the house and carried them to the stables. Esperanza stood in the middle of it all, watching the outline of her home silhouetted in flames against the night sky. Someone wrapped a blanket around her. Was she cold? She did not know.

Miguel ran out of the burning house carrying

Abuelita in his arms. He laid her down and Hortensia screamed. The back of his shirt was on fire. Alfonso tackled him, rolling him over and over on the ground until the fire was out. Miguel stood up and slowly took off the blackened shirt. He wasn't badly burned.

Mama cradled Abuelita in her arms.

"Mama," said Esperanza, "Is she . . . ?"

"No, she is alive, but weak and her ankle . . . I don't think she can walk," said Mama.

Esperanza knelt down.

"Abuelita, where were you?"

Her grandmother held up the cloth bag with her crocheting and after some minutes of coughing, whispered, "We must have something to do while we wait."

The fire's anger could not be contained. It spread to the grapes. The flames ran along the deliberate rows of the vines, like long curved fingers reaching for the horizon, lighting the night sky.

Esperanza stood as if in a trance and watched El Rancho de las Rosas burn.

Mama, Abuelita, and Esperanza slept in the servants' cabins. They really didn't sleep much, but they didn't cry either. They were numb, as if encased in a thick skin that nothing could penetrate. And there was no point in talking about how it happened. They all knew that the uncles had arranged the fire.

At dawn, still in her nightgown, Esperanza went out among the rubble. Avoiding the smoldering piles, she picked through the black wood, hoping to find something to salvage. She sat on an adobe block near what used to be the front door, and looked over at Papa's rose garden. Flowerless stems were covered in soot. Dazed and hugging herself, Esperanza surveyed the surviving victims: the twisted forms of wrought-iron chairs, unharmed cast-iron skillets, and the mortars and pestles from the kitchen that were made from lava rock and refused to burn. Then she saw the remains of the trunk that used to sit at the foot of her bed, the metal straps still intact. She stood up and hurried toward it, hoping for *un milagro*, a miracle. She looked closely, but all that remained were black cinders.

There was nothing left inside, for someday.

~

Esperanza saw her uncles approaching on horseback and ran to tell the others. Mama waited on the steps of the cabin with her arms crossed, looking like a fierce statue. Alfonso, Hortensia, and Miguel stood nearby.

"Ramona," said Tío Marco, remaining on his horse. "Another sadness in so short a time. We are deeply sorry."

"I have come to give you another chance," said Tío Luis. "If you reconsider my proposal, I will build a bigger, more beautiful house and I will replant everything. Of course, if you prefer, you can live here with the servants, as long as another tragedy does not happen to their homes as well. There is no main house or fields where they can work, so you see that many people's lives and jobs depend upon you. And I am sure you want the best for Esperanza, do you not?"

Mama did not speak for several moments. She looked around at the servants who had gathered. Now, her face did not seem so fierce and her eyes were damp. Esperanza wondered where the servants would go when Mama told Tío Luis no.

Mama looked at Esperanza with eyes that said, "forgive me." Then she dropped her head and stared at the ground. "I will consider your proposal," said Mama.

Tío Luis smiled. "I am delighted! I have no doubt that you will make the right decision. I will be back in a few days for your answer."

"Mama, no!" said Esperanza. She turned to Tío Luis and said, "I hate you!"

Tío Luis ignored her. "And Ramona, if Esperanza is to be my daughter, she must have better manners. In fact, today I will look into boarding schools where they can teach her to act like a lady." Then he turned his horse, dug his spurs into the animal, and rode away.

Esperanza began to weep. She grabbed Mama's arm and said, "Why? Why did you tell him that?"

But Mama was not listening to her. She was looking up, as if consulting the angels.

Finally, she said, "Alfonso. Hortensia. We must talk with Abuelita. Esperanza and Miguel, come inside, you are old enough to hear the discussions."

"But Mama . . ."

Mama took Esperanza by the shoulders and faced her. "*Mija*, my daughter, do not worry. I know what I am doing."

⁓

They all crowded into Hortensia and Alfonso's tiny bedroom where Abuelita was resting, her swollen ankle propped on pillows. Esperanza sat on Abuelita's bed while Mama and the others stood.

"Alfonso, what are my options?" said Mama.

"If you don't intend to marry him, Señora, you cannot stay here. He would burn down the servants' quarters next. There will be no income because there are no grapes. You would have to depend on the charity of others, and they would be afraid to help you. You could move to some other part of Mexico, but in poverty. Luis's influence is far-reaching."

The room was quiet. Mama looked out the window and tapped her fingers on the wooden sill.

Hortensia went to Mama's side and touched her arm. "You should know that we have decided to go to the United States. Alfonso's brother has been writing to us about the big farm in California where he works now. He can arrange jobs and a cabin for us, too. We are sending the letter tomorrow."

Mama turned and looked at Abuelita. With no words spoken, Abuelita nodded.

"What if Esperanza and I went with you? To the United States," said Mama.

"Mama, we cannot leave Abuelita!"

Abuelita put her hand on Esperanza's. "I would come later, when I am stronger."

"But my friends and my school. We can't just leave! And Papa, what would he think?"

"What should we do, Esperanza? Do you think Papa would want me to marry Tío Luis and let him send you to a school in another city?"

Esperanza felt confused. Her uncle said he would replace everything as it was. But she could not imagine Mama being married to anyone but Papa. She looked at Mama's face and saw sadness, worry, and pain. Mama would do anything for her. But if Mama married Tío Luis, she knew that everything would not really be as it was. Tío Luis would send her away and she and Mama wouldn't even be together.

"No," she whispered.

"You are sure that you want to go with us?" said Hortensia.

"I am sure," said Mama, her voice stronger. "But crossing the border is more difficult these days. You have your papers but ours were lost in the fire and they forbid anyone to enter without a visa."

"I will arrange it," said Abuelita. "My sisters,

in the convent. They can discreetly get you duplicates."

"No one could know about this, Señora," said Alfonso. "We would all have to keep it a secret if you come. This will be a great insult to Luis. If he finds out, he will prevent you from leaving the territory."

A tiny smile appeared on Mama's tired face. "Yes, it would be a great insult to him, wouldn't it?"

"In California there is only fieldwork," said Miguel.

"I am stronger than you think," said Mama.

"We will help each other." Hortensia put her arm around Mama.

Abuelita squeezed Esperanza's hand. "Do not be afraid to start over. When I was your age, I left Spain with my mother, father, and sisters. A Mexican official had offered my father a job here in Mexico. So we came. We had to take several ships and the journey lasted months. When we arrived, nothing was as promised. There were many hard times. But life was also exciting. And we had each other. Esperanza, do you remember the story of the phoenix, the lovely young bird that is re-born from its own ashes?"

Esperanza nodded. Abuelita had read it to her many times from a book of myths.

"We are like the phoenix," said Abuelita. "Rising again, with a new life ahead of us."

When she realized she was crying, Esperanza wiped her eyes with her shawl. Yes, she thought. They could have a home in California. A beautiful home. Alfonso and Hortensia and Miguel could take care of them and they'd be rid of the uncles. And Abuelita would join them, as soon as she was well. Still sniffling and caught up in their affection and strength, Esperanza said, "And . . . and I could work, too."

They all looked at her.

And for the first time since Papa died, everyone laughed.

⌒

The next day Abuelita's sisters came for her in a wagon. The nuns, dressed in their black and white habits, gently lifted Abuelita into the back. They pulled a blanket under her chin and Esperanza went to her and held her hand. She remembered the night that Alfonso and Miguel brought Papa home in the wagon. How long ago was that? She knew that it had only been a few weeks, but it seemed like many lifetimes ago.

Esperanza tenderly hugged and kissed Abuelita.

"Mi nieta, we won't be able to communicate. The mail is unpredictable and I'm sure your uncles will be watching my correspondence. But I will come, of that you can be certain. While you are waiting, finish this for me." She handed Esperanza the bundle of crocheting. "Look at the zigzag of the blanket. Mountains and valleys. Right now you are in the bottom of the valley and your problems loom big around you. But soon, you will be at the top of a mountain again. After you have lived many mountains and valleys, we will be together."

Through her tears Esperanza said, "Please get well. Please come to us."

"I promise. And you promise to take care of Mama for me."

Next it was Mama's turn. Esperanza could not watch. She buried her head in Hortensia's shoulder until she heard the wagon pulling away. Then she went to Mama and put her arms around her. They watched the wagon disappear down the path until it was a speck in the distance, until even the dust was gone.

That's when Esperanza noticed the old trunk with the leather straps that the nuns had left.

"What is in the trunk?" she asked.

"Our papers to travel. And clothes from the poor box at the convent."

"The poor box?"

"People donate them," said Mama, "for others who cannot afford to buy their own."

"Mama, at a time like this, must we worry about some poor family who needs clothes?"

"Esperanza," said Mama. "We have little money and Hortensia, Alfonso, and Miguel are no longer our servants. We are indebted to *them* for our finances and our future. And that trunk of clothes for the poor? Esperanza, it is for us."

~

Señor Rodríguez was the only person they could trust. He came after dark for secret meetings, always carrying a basket of figs for the grieving family to disguise his real reason for visiting. Esperanza fell asleep each night on a blanket on the floor, listening to the adults' hushed voices and mysterious plans. And smelling the plentiful piles of white figs that she knew would never be eaten.

At the end of the week Esperanza was sitting on the small step to Hortensia and Alfonso's cabin when Tío Luis rode up. He remained on his horse and sent Alfonso to bring Mama.

In a few moments, Mama walked toward them, drying her hands on her apron. She held her head high and looked beautiful, even dressed in the old clothes from the poor box.

"Luis, I have considered your proposal and in

the interest of the servants and Esperanza, I will marry you, in due time. But you must begin replanting and rebuilding immediately, as the servants need their jobs."

Esperanza was quiet and stared at the dirt, hiding the smirk on her face.

Tío Luis could not contain his grin. He sat up straighter. "I knew you would come to your senses, Ramona. I will announce the engagement at once."

Mama nodded, almost bowing. "One more thing," she said. "We will need a wagon to visit Abuelita. She is at the convent in La Purísima. I must see to her every few weeks."

"I will send one over this afternoon," said Tío Luis, smiling. "A new one. And those clothes, Ramona! They are not fitting for a woman of your stature, and Esperanza looks like a waif. I will send a dressmaker next week with new fabrics."

In the nicest way possible, Esperanza looked up and said, "Thank you, Tío Luis. I am happy that you will be taking care of us."

"Yes, of course," he said, not even glancing at her.

Esperanza smiled at him anyway, because she knew she would never spend a night in the same house with him and he would never be her step-father. She almost wished she would be able to see his face when he realized that they had escaped. He wouldn't be grinning like a proud rooster then.

～

The night before the dressmaker was scheduled to come, Mama woke Esperanza in the middle of the night, and they left with only what they could carry. Esperanza held a valise filled with clothes, a small package of *tamales*, and her doll from Papa. She and Mama and Hortensia were wrapped in dark shawls to blend in with the night.

They could not take a chance of walking on the roads, so Miguel and Alfonso led them through the grape rows, weaving across Papa's land toward the Rodríguez ranch. There was

enough moonlight so that they could see the out-
lines of the twisted and charred trunks, the burnt-
out vines rolling in parallel lines toward the
mountains. It looked as if someone had taken a giant comb, dipped it in black paint, and gently
swirled it across a huge canvas.

They reached the fig orchard that separated
Papa's land from Señor Rodríguez's. Alfonso, Hortensia, and Miguel walked ahead. But Esperanza
held back, and pulled on Mama's hand to keep
her there for a moment. They turned to look at
what used to be El Rancho de las Rosas in the
distance.

Sadness and anger tangled in Esperanza's stomach as she thought of all that she was leaving: her
friends and her school, her life as it once was,
Abuelita. And Papa. She felt as though she was
leaving him, too.

As if reading her mind, Mama said, "Papa's
heart will find us wherever we go." Then Mama
took a determined breath and headed toward the
sprawling trees.

Esperanza followed but hesitated every few

56

steps, looking back. She hated leaving, but how could she stay?

With each stride, Papa's land became smaller and smaller. She hurried after Mama, knowing that she might never come back to her home again, and her heart filled with venom for Tío Luis. When she turned around one last time, she could see nothing behind her but a trail of splattered figs she had resentfully smashed beneath her feet.

# LAS GUAYABAS
### G U A V A S

They emerged from the fig orchard and contin-ued through a pear grove. When they came into a clearing, they saw Señor Rodríguez waiting with a lantern by the barn doors. They hurried inside. Pigeons fluttered in the rafters. Their wagon was waiting, surrounded by crates of green guavas.

"Did Marisol come?" asked Esperanza, her eyes searching the barn.

"I could tell no one about your departure," said Señor Rodríguez. "When the time is right, I will tell her that you looked for her and said good-bye. Now we must hurry. You need the protection of darkness."

Alfonso, Miguel, and Señor Rodríguez had built another floor in the wagon, higher than the real one and open at the back, with barely enough room be-tween for Mama, Esperanza, and Hortensia to lie down. Hortensia lined it with blankets.

58

Esperanza had known about the plan, but now she hesitated when she saw the small space.

"Please, can I sit with Alfonso and Miguel?"

"Mija, it is necessary," said Mama.

"There are too many bandits," said Alfonso. "It is not safe for women to be on the roads at night. Besides, your uncles have many spies. Remember? That is why we must take the wagon to Zacatecas and catch the train there, instead of from Aguas-calientes."

"Luis has bragged about the engagement to everyone," said Hortensia. "Think how angry he will be when he discovers you have gone. We cannot take the chance of you being seen."

Mama and Hortensia said grateful good-byes to Señor Rodríguez, then slid between the floors of the wagon.

Esperanza reluctantly scooted on her back be-tween them. "When can we get out?"

"Every few hours, we will stop and stretch," said Mama.

Esperanza stared at the wood planks just a few inches from her face. She could hear Alfonso,

Miguel, and Señor Rodríguez dumping crate after crate of guavas onto the floor above them, the almost-ripe fruit rolling and tumbling as it was piled on. The guavas smelled fresh and sweet, like pears and oranges all in one. Then she felt the guavas roll in around her feet as Alfonso and Miguel covered the opening. If anyone saw the wagon on the road, it would look like a farmer and his son, taking a load of fruit to market.

"How are you?" Alfonso asked, sounding far away.

"We are fine," called Hortensia.

The wagon pulled out of the barn and the guavas shifted, then settled. It was dark inside and it felt like someone was rocking them in a bumpy cradle, sometimes side to side and sometimes back and forth. Esperanza began to feel frightened. She knew that with a few kicks of her feet she could get out, but still she felt trapped. Suddenly, she thought she couldn't breathe.

"Mama!" she said, gasping for air.

"Right here, Esperanza. Everything is fine."

"Do you remember," said Hortensia, taking her hand, "when you were only five years old and we hid from the thieves? You were so brave for such a little girl. Your parents and Alfonso and the other servants had gone to town. It was just you and me and Miguel in the house. We were in your bedroom and I was pinning the hem of your beautiful blue silk dress. Do you remember that dress? You wanted it pinned higher so your new shoes would show."

Esperanza's eyes were beginning to adjust to the darkness and to the pitch and roll of the wagon. "Miguel ran into the house because he had seen bandits," said Esperanza, exhaling. She remembered standing on a chair with her arms outstretched like a bird ready for flight while Hortensia fitted the sides of the dress. And she remembered the new shoes, shiny and black.

"Yes," said Hortensia. "I looked out the window to see six men, their faces covered with handkerchiefs, and they all held rifles. They were renegades who thought they had permission to steal from the rich and give to the poor. But they didn't always give to the poor and they sometimes killed innocent people."

"We hid under the bed," said Esperanza. "And we pulled down the bedcovers so they couldn't see us." She remembered staring straight up at the bed boards. Much like the boards enclosing them in the wagon now. She took another long breath.

"What we didn't know was that Miguel had a big field mouse in his pocket," said Hortensia.

"Yes. He was going to scare me with it," said Esperanza.

The wagon creaked and swayed. They could hear Alfonso and Miguel murmuring above them. The persistent smell of the guavas filled their noses. Esperanza relaxed a little.

Hortensia continued. "The men came into the house and we could hear them opening cupboards and stealing the silver. Then we heard them climb the stairs. Two men came into the bedroom and we saw their big boots through a crack in the bedcover. But we didn't say a word."

"Until a pin poked me and I moved my leg and made a noise."

"I was so frightened they would find us," said Hortensia.

"But Miguel pushed the mouse out from under the bed and it ran around the room. The men were startled but started laughing. And then one of them said, 'It is just a *ratón*. We've got plenty. Let's go,' and they left," said Esperanza.

Mama said, "They took almost all of the silver, but Papa and I only cared that all of you were safe. Do you remember how Papa said that Miguel was very smart and brave and asked him what he wanted for protecting you, his most prized possession?"

Esperanza remembered. "Miguel wanted to go on a train ride."

Hortensia started to hum softly and Mama held Esperanza's hand.

Miguel's reward, that day-long train ride to Zacatecas, seemed like yesterday. Miguel had been eight and Esperanza five. She wore the beautiful blue silk dress and could still see Miguel standing at the station, wearing a bow tie and practically shining, as if Hortensia had cleaned and starched his entire body. Even his hair was slicked down smooth and his eyes gleamed with excitement. He was mesmerized by the locomotive, watching it slowly pull in. Esperanza had been excited, too.

When the train arrived, all sputtering and blustery, porters had hurried to escort them, showing them the way to their car. Papa took her hand and Miguel's and they boarded, waving good-bye to Alfonso and Hortensia. The compartment had seats of soft leather, and she and Miguel had bounced happily upon them. Later, they ate in the dining car at little tables covered in white linens and set with silver and crystal. When the waiter came and asked if there was anything he could bring them, Esperanza said, "Yes, please bring lunch, now." The men and women dressed in their hats and fancy clothes smiled and chuckled at what must have looked like a doting father and two privileged children. When they arrived in Zacatecas, a woman wrapped in a colorful *rebozo,* a blanket shawl, boarded the train selling mangoes on a stick. The mangoes were peeled and carved to look like exotic flowers. Papa bought one for each of them. On the return ride, she and Miguel, with their noses pressed against the window, and their hands still sticky from the fresh mango, had waved to every person they saw.

The wagon jostled them now as it hit a hole in the road. Esperanza wished she could get to Zacatecas as fast as she had that day on the train instead of traveling on back roads, hidden in a slow wagon. But this time, she was buried beneath a mountain of guavas and could not wave to anyone. There was no comfort. And there was no Papa.

⁓

Esperanza stood at the station in Zacatecas, tugging at the second-hand dress. It didn't fit properly and was the most awful yellow. And even though they had been out of the wagon for some hours, she still smelled like guavas.

It had taken them two days to arrive in

Zacatecas, but finally, that morning, they left the wagon hidden in a thicket of shrubs and trees and walked into town. After the discomfort of the wagon, she was looking forward to the train.

The locomotive arrived pulling a line of cars and hissing and spewing steam. But they did not board the fancy car with the compartments and leather seats or the dining car with the white linens. Instead, Alfonso led them to a car with rows of wooden benches, like church pews facing each other, already crowded with peasants. Trash littered the floor and it reeked of rotting fruit and urine. A man with a small goat on his lap grinned at Esperanza, revealing no teeth. Three barefoot children, two boys and a girl, crowded near their mother. Their legs were chalky with dust, their clothes were in tatters, and their hair was grimy. An old, frail beggar woman pushed by them to the back of the car, clutching a picture of Our Lady of Guadalupe. Her hand was outstretched for alms.

Esperanza had never been so close to so many peasants before. When she went to school, all of her friends were like her. When she went to town, she was escorted and hurried around any beggars. And the peasants always kept their distance. That was simply the way it was. She couldn't help but wonder if they would steal her things.

"Mama," said Esperanza, stopping in the doorway. "We cannot travel in this car. It . . . it is not clean. And the people do not look trustworthy."

Esperanza saw Miguel frown as he edged around her to sit down.

Mama took her hand and guided her to an empty bench where Esperanza slid over next to the window. "Papa would never have had us sit here and Abuelita wouldn't approve," she said, stubbornly.

"Mija, it is all we can afford," said Mama. "We must make do. It is not easy for me either. But remember, we are going to a place that will be better than living with Tío Luis, and at least we will be together."

The train pulled out and settled into a steady motion. Hortensia and Mama took out their crocheting. Mama was using a small hook and white cotton thread to make *carpetas*, lace doilies, to put under a lamp or a vase. She held up her work to Esperanza and smiled. "Would you like to learn?"

Esperanza shook her head. Why did Mama bother crocheting lace? They had no vases or *lámparas* to put on top of them. Esperanza leaned her head against the window. She knew she did not belong here. She was Esperanza Ortega from El Rancho de las Rosas. She crossed her arms tight and stared out the window.

For hours, Esperanza watched the undulating land pass in front of her. Everything seemed to remind her of what she had left behind: the *nopales* reminded her of Abuelita who loved to eat the prickly pear cactus sliced and soaked in vinegar and oil; the dogs from small villages that barked and ran after the train reminded her of Marisol, whose dog, Capitán, chased after trains the same way. And every time Esperanza saw a shrine decorated with crosses, flowers, and miniature statues of saints next to the rails, she couldn't help but wonder if it had been someone's father who had died on the tracks and if somewhere there was another girl who missed him, too.

Esperanza opened her valise to check on the doll, lifting it out and straightening her clothes. The barefoot peasant girl ran over.

"*Mona*," she said, and reached up to touch the doll. Esperanza quickly jerked it away and put it back in the valise, covering it with the old clothes.

"¡*Mona*! ¡*Mona*!" said the little girl, running back to her mother. And then she began to cry.

Mama and Hortensia both stopped their needles and stared at Esperanza.

Mama looked across at the girl's mother. "I am sorry for my daughter's bad manners."

Esperanza looked at Mama in surprise. Why was she apologizing to these people? She and Mama shouldn't even be sitting in this car.

Hortensia looked from one to the other and excused herself. "I think I will find Alfonso and Miguel and see if they bought *tortillas* at the station."

Mama looked at Esperanza. "I don't think it would have hurt to let her hold it for a few moments."

"Mama, she is poor and dirty . . ." said Esperanza.

But Mama interrupted. "When you scorn these people, you scorn Miguel, Hortensia, and Alfonso. And you embarrass me and yourself. As difficult as it is to accept, our lives are different now."

The child kept crying. Her face was so dirty that her tears washed clean streaks down her cheeks. Esperanza suddenly felt ashamed and the color rose in her face, but she still pushed the valise farther under the seat with her feet and turned her body away from Mama.

Esperanza tried not to look back at the little girl but she couldn't help it. She wished she could tell the little girl's mother that she had always given her old toys to the orphanage, but that this doll was special. Besides, the child would have soiled it with her hands.

Mama reached in her bag and pulled out a ball of blanket yarn. "Esperanza, hold out your hands for me." She raised her eyebrows and nodded toward the girl. Esperanza knew exactly what Mama intended to do. They had done it many times before.

Mama wrapped the yarn around Esperanza's outstretched hands about fifty times until they were almost covered. Then she slipped a string of yarn through the middle of the loops and tied a tight knot before Esperanza removed her hands. A few inches below the knot, Mama tied another snug knot around all the yarn, forming a head. Then she cut the bottom loops, separated the strands into sections, and braided each section into what looked like arms and legs. She held the yarn doll up, offering it to the little girl. She ran to Mama, smiling, took the doll, and ran back to her own mother's side.

The mother whispered into the girl's ear.

Shyly, she said, "*Gracias*. Thank you."

"*De nada*. You're welcome," said Mama.

The woman and the children got off the train at the next stop. Esperanza watched the little girl stop in front of their window, wave to Mama, and smile again. Before she walked away, she made the yarn doll wave good-bye, too.

Esperanza was glad the girl got off the train and took the silly yarn doll with her. Otherwise, she would have been reminded of her own selfishness and Mama's disapproval for miles to come.

~

*Clicketta, clicketta, clicketta.* The song of the locomotive was monotonous as they traveled north, and the hours seemed like Mama's never-ending ball of thread unwinding in front of them. Each morning the sun peeked over one spur of the Sierra Madre, sometimes shining through pine trees. In the evening, it set on the left, sinking behind another peak and leaving pink clouds and purple mountains against the darkening sky. When people got on and off, Esperanza and the others changed their seats. When the car filled up, they sometimes stood. When the car was less crowded, they put their valises under their heads and tried to sleep on the benches.

At every stop, Miguel and Alfonso hurried off

the train with a package. From the window, Esperanza watched them go to a water trough, unwrap an oilcloth, and dampen the bundle inside. Then they would wrap it in the oilcloth again, board the train, and put it carefully back into Alfonso's bag.

"What is in there?" Esperanza finally asked Alfonso, as the train pulled away from yet another station.

"You will see when we get there." He smiled and a knowing look passed between him and Miguel.

Esperanza was annoyed with Alfonso for taking the package on and off the train without telling her what was inside. She was tired of Hortensia's humming and weary of watching Mama crochet, as if nothing unusual were happening to them. But most of all she was bored with Miguel's constant talk about trains. He chatted with the conductors. He got off at every stop and watched the engineers. He studied the train schedule and wanted to report it all to Esperanza. He seemed as happy as Esperanza was irritable.

"When I get to California, I am going to work for the railroad," said Miguel, looking anxiously toward the horizon. They had spread pieces of brown paper in their laps and were eating *pepinos*, cucumbers sprinkled with salt and ground *chiles*.

"I'm thirsty. Are they selling juice in the other car?" asked Esperanza.

"I would have worked at the railroad in Mexico," continued Miguel, as if Esperanza had not tried to change the subject. "But it is not easy to get a job in Mexico. You need *una palanca*, a lever, to get a job at the railroads. I had no connections but your father did. Since I was a small boy, he gave me his word that he would help me. And he would have kept his promise. He . . . he always kept his promises to me."

At the mention of Papa, Esperanza felt that sinking feeling again. She looked at Miguel. He quickly turned his head away from her and looked hard out the window, but she saw that his eyes were damp. She had never thought about how much her papa must have meant to Miguel. It dawned on her that even though Miguel was a servant, Papa may have thought of him as the son he never had. But Papa's influence was gone. What would happen to Miguel's dreams now?

"And in the United States?" she asked quietly.

"I hear that in the United States, you do not need *una palanca*. That even the poorest man can become rich if he works hard enough."

⌒

They had been on the train for four days and nights when a woman got on with a wire cage containing six red hens. The chickens squawked and cackled and when they flapped their wings, tiny russet feathers floated around the car. The woman sat opposite Mama and Hortensia and within minutes she had told them that her name was Carmen, that her husband had died and left her with eight children, and that she had been at her brother's house helping his family with a new baby.

"Would you like *dulces*, sweets?" she asked Esperanza, holding open a bag.

Esperanza looked at Mama, who smiled and nodded her approval.

Esperanza hesitantly reached inside and took out a square of coconut candy. Mama had never permitted her to take candy from someone she didn't know before, especially from a poor person.

"Señora, why do you travel with the hens?" asked Mama.

"I sell eggs to feed my family. My brother raises hens and he gave these to me."

"And you can support your large family that way?" asked Hortensia.

Carmen smiled. "I am poor, but I am rich. I have my children, I have a garden with roses, and I have my faith and the memories of those who have gone before me. What more is there?"

Hortensia and Mama smiled, nodding their heads. And after a few thoughtful moments, Mama was blotting away stray tears.

The three women continued talking as the train passed fields of corn, orange orchards, and cows grazing on rolling hills. They talked as the train traveled through small towns, where peasant children ran after the caboose, just for the sake of running. Soon, Mama was confiding in Carmen, telling her all that had happened with Papa and Tío Luis. Carmen listened and made clucking noises like one of her hens, as if she understood Mama's and Esperanza's problems. Esperanza looked from Mama to Carmen to Hortensia. She was amazed at how easily Carmen had plopped herself down and had plunged into intimate conversation. It didn't seem correct somehow. Mama had always been so proper and concerned about what was said and not said. In Aguascalientes, she would have thought it was "inappropriate" to tell an egg woman their problems, yet now she didn't hesitate.

"Mama," whispered Esperanza, taking on a tone she had heard Mama use many times. "Do you think it is *wise* to tell a peasant our personal business?"

Mama tried not to smile. She whispered back, "It is all right, Esperanza, because now we are peasants, too."

Esperanza ignored Mama's comment. What was wrong with her? Had all of Mama's rules changed since they had boarded this train?

When they pulled into Carmen's town, Mama gave her three of the beautiful lace *carpetas* she had made. "For your house," she said.

Carmen gave Mama two chickens, in an old shopping bag that she tied with string. "For your future," she said.

Then Mama, Hortensia, and Carmen hugged as if they had been friends forever.

"*Buena suerte,* good luck," they said to one another.

Alfonso and Miguel helped Carmen with her packages and the cage of chickens. When Miguel got back on the train, he sat next to Esperanza, near the window. They watched Carmen greet her waiting children, several of the little ones scrambling into her arms.

In front of the station, a crippled Indian woman crawled on her knees, her hand outstretched toward a group of ladies and gentlemen who were finely dressed in clothes like the ones that used to hang in Esperanza's and Mama's closets. The people turned their backs on the begging woman but Carmen walked over and gave her a coin and some *tortillas* from her bag. The woman blessed her, making the sign of the cross. Then Carmen took her children's hands and walked away.

"She has eight children and sells eggs to survive. Yet when she can barely afford it she gave your mother two hens and helped the crippled woman," said Miguel. "The rich take care of the rich and the poor take care of those who have less than they have."

"But why does Carmen need to take care of the beggar at all?" said Esperanza. "Look. Only a few yards away is the farmer's market with carts of fresh food."

Miguel looked at Esperanza, wrinkled his forehead, and shook his head. "There is a Mexican saying: 'Full bellies and Spanish blood go hand in hand.'"

Esperanza looked at him and raised her eyebrows.

"Have you never noticed?" he said, sounding surprised. "Those with Spanish blood, who have the fairest complexions in the land, are the wealthiest."

Esperanza suddenly felt guilty and did not want to admit that she had never noticed or that it might be true. Besides, they were going to the United States now and it certainly would not be true there.

Esperanza shrugged. "It is just something that old wives say."

"No," said Miguel. "It is something the poor say."

# LOS MELONES
## CANTALOUPES

They reached the border at Mexicali in the morning. Finally, the train stopped moving and everyone disembarked. The land was dry and the panorama was barren except for date palms, cactus, and an occasional squirrel or road-runner. The conductors herded everyone into a building where they stood in long lines waiting to pass through immigration. Esperanza noticed that the people in the first cars were escorted to the shortest lines and passed through quickly.

Inside, the air was stagnant and thick with the smell of body odor. Esperanza and Mama, their faces shiny with grime and perspiration, looked tired and wilted and they slumped with even the slight weight of their valises. The closer Esperanza got to the front, the more nervous she became. She looked at her papers and hoped they were in order. What if the officials found something wrong? Would they send her back to her uncles? Would they arrest her and put her in jail?

She reached the desk and handed over the documents.

The immigration official seemed angry for no reason. "Where are you coming from?"

She looked at Mama who was behind her.

"We are from Aguascalientes," said Mama, stepping forward.

"And what is your purpose for entering the United States?"

Esperanza was afraid to speak. What if she said the wrong thing?

"To work," said Mama, handing him her documents as well.

"What work?" demanded the man.

Mama's demeanor changed. She stood up straight and tall and deliberately blotted her face with a handkerchief. She looked directly into the official's eyes and spoke calmly as if she were giving simple directions to a servant. "I am sure you can see that everything is in order. The name of the employer is written there. People are expecting us."

The man studied Mama. He looked at their faces, then the pages, then their faces again.

Standing tall and proud, Mama never took her eyes from his face.

Why was it taking so long?

Finally, he grabbed the stamp and pounded each page with the words "Mexican National." He shoved their papers at them and waved them through. Mama took Esperanza's hand and hurried her toward another train.

They boarded and waited an hour for all the passengers to get through immigration. Esperanza looked out the window. Across the tracks, several groups of people were being prodded onto another train headed back toward Mexico.

"My heart aches for those people. They came all this way just to be sent back," said Mama.

"But why?" asked Esperanza.

"Many reasons. They had no papers, false ones, or no proof of work. Or there might have been a problem with just one member of the family so they all chose to go back instead of being separated."

Esperanza thought about being separated from Mama and gratefully took her hand and squeezed it.

Almost everyone had boarded except Alfonso, Hortensia, and Miguel. Esperanza kept looking for them, and she became more anxious with each passing minute. "Mama, where are they?"

Mama said nothing but Esperanza could see worry in her eyes, too.

Finally, Hortensia got on. The train's engines began to chug.

Her voice tense, Esperanza said, "What happened to Alfonso and Miguel?"

Hortensia pointed out the window. "They had to find some water."

Alfonso was running toward the train with Miguel close behind, waving the secret package and grinning. The train slowly started moving as they hopped on.

Esperanza wanted to be angry at them for

making her anxious. She wanted to yell at them for waiting until the very last minute just so they could find water for their package that was probably nonsense anyway. But looking from one to the other, she sat back, limp with relief, happy to have them all together surrounding her, and surprised that she could be so glad to be back on the train.

~

"Anza, we're here. Wake up!"

She sat up groggily, barely opening her eyes. "What day is this?" she asked.

"You've been asleep for hours. Wake up! It is Thursday. And we are here in Los Angeles!"

"Look, there they are!" said Alfonso, pointing out the window. "My brother, Juan, and Josefina, his wife. And his children, Isabel and the twins. They have all come."

A *campesino* family waved to them. Juan and Josefina each held a baby about a year old in their arms. It was easy to see that the man was Alfonso's brother, even though he didn't have a mustache.

Josefina was plump with a round face and a complexion that was fairer than Esperanza's. She was smiling and waving with her free hand. Next to her stood a girl about eight years old, wearing a dress that was too big and shoes with no socks. Delicate and frail, with big brown eyes, long braids, and skinny legs, she looked like a young deer. Esperanza couldn't help but think how much she looked like the doll Papa had given her.

There was much hugging among all the relatives.

Alfonso said, "Everyone, this is Señora Ortega and Esperanza."

"Alfonso, please call me Ramona."

"Yes, of course, Señora. My family feels like they know you because we have all written letters about you for years."

Mama hugged Juan and Josefina and said, "Thank you for all you have done for us already."

Miguel teased his cousin, pulling her braids. "Esperanza, this is Isabel."

Isabel looked at Esperanza, her eyes wide with wonder, and in a voice that was soft and whispery said, "Were you really so very wealthy? Did you always get your way, and have all the dolls and fancy dresses you wanted?"

Esperanza's mouth pressed into an irritated line. She could only imagine the letters Miguel had written. Had he told Isabel that in Mexico they stood on different sides of the river?

"The truck is this way," said Juan. "We have a long ride."

Esperanza picked up her valise and followed Isabel's father. She looked around and was relieved to see that compared to the desert, Los Angeles had lush palms and green grass and even though it was September, roses were still blooming in the flower beds. She took a deep breath. The aroma of oranges from a nearby grove was reassuring and familiar. Maybe it wouldn't be so different here.

Juan, Josefina, Mama, and Hortensia crowded onto the front seat of the rickety truck. Isabel, Esperanza, Alfonso, and Miguel sat in the truck bed with the babies and the two red hens. The vehicle looked like it should be hauling animals instead of people, but Esperanza had said nothing to Mama. Besides, after so many days on the train, it felt good to stretch out her legs.

The old jalopy rocked and swayed as it climbed out of the San Fernando Valley, weaving up through hills covered with dried-out shrubs. She sat with her back against the cab and the hot wind whipped her loose hair. Alfonso tied a blanket across the wooden slats to make a canopy of shade.

The babies, Lupe and Pepe, a girl and a boy, were dark-eyed cherubs, with thick mops of black hair. Esperanza was surprised at how much they looked alike; the only difference was the tiny gold earrings in Lupe's ears. Pepe crawled into Esperanza's lap and Lupe into Isabel's. When the baby fell asleep against Esperanza, his head slid down her arm, leaving a stream of perspiration. "Is it always so hot here?" she asked.

"My papa says it is the dry air that makes it so hot and sometimes it is even hotter," said Isabel. "But it is better than living in El Centro because now we do not have to live in a tent."

"A tent?"

"Last year we worked for another farm in El Centro in the Imperial Valley, not too far from the border. We were there during the melons. We lived in a tent with a dirt floor and had to carry water. We cooked outside. But then we moved north to Arvin. That's where we're going now. A big company owns the camp. We pay seven dollars a month and my papa says it is worth it to have piped-in cold water and electricity and a kitchen inside. He says the farm is six thousand acres." Isabel leaned toward Esperanza and grinned as if she were telling a big secret. "And a school. Next week, I get to go to school, and I will learn to read. Can you read?"

"Of course," said Esperanza.

"Will you go to school?" asked Isabel.

"I went to private school and started when I was four so I have already passed through level eight. When my grandmother comes, maybe I will go to high school."

"Well, when I go to school, I will learn in English," said Isabel.

Esperanza nodded and tried to smile back. Isabel was so happy, she thought, about such little things.

The brown, barren mountains rose higher and a red-tailed hawk seemed to follow them for miles. The truck rattled up a steep grade past sparse, dry canyons and Esperanza's ears began to feel full and tight. "How much longer?"

"We will stop for lunch soon," said Isabel.

They wove through the golden hills, softly sculpted with rounded tops, until Juan finally slowed the truck and turned down a side road. When they came to an area shaded by a single tree, they piled out of the truck and Josefina spread a blanket on the ground, then unwrapped a bundle of *burritos*, avocados, and grapes. They sat in the shade and ate. Mama, Hortensia, and Josefina chatted and watched the babies while Isabel lay down on the blanket between Alfonso and Juan. She was soon asleep.

Esperanza wandered away from the group, grateful not to be rocking in a truck or a train. She walked to an overlook. Below, canyons plunged to an *arroyo*, a silver line of water from an unknown river. It was quiet and peaceful here, the sweet silence broken only by the swish of dried grasses from the wind.

With her feet solid on the ground for the first time in many days, Esperanza remembered what Papa had taught her when she was little: If she lay on the land, and was very still and quiet, she could hear the heartbeat of the valley.

"Can I hear it from here, Papa?"

She stretched out on her stomach and reached her arms to the side, hugging the earth. She let the stillness settle upon her and listened.

She heard nothing.

Be patient, she reminded herself, and the fruit will fall into your hand.

She listened again, but the heartbeat was not there. She tried one more time, desperately wanting to hear it. But there was no reassuring thump repeating itself. No sound of the earth's heartbeat. Or Papa's. There was only the prickly sound of dry grass.

Determined, Esperanza pressed her ear harder

to the ground. "I can't hear it!" She pounded the earth. "Let me hear it." Tears burst from her eyes as if someone had squeezed an overripe orange. Confusion and uncertainty spilled forth and became an *arroyo* of their own.

She rolled on her back, her tears worming down her face into her ears. Seeing nothing but the vast sky in dizzying swirls of blue and white, she began to feel as if she were floating and drifting upward. She lifted higher and part of her liked the sensation but another part of her felt untethered and frightened. She tried to find the place in her heart where her life was anchored, but she couldn't, so she closed her eyes and pressed the palms of her hands against the earth, making sure it was there. She felt as if she were falling, careening through the hot air. Her skin perspired and she felt cold and nauseous. She took short breaths, heaving in and out.

Suddenly, the world went black.

Someone hovered over her.

She sat up quickly. How long had she been in the darkness? She held her pounding chest and looked up at Miguel.

"Anza, are you all right?"

She took a deep breath and brushed off her dress. Had she really floated above the earth? Had Miguel seen her? She knew her face was red and blotchy. "I'm fine," she said quickly, wiping the tears from her face. "Don't tell Mama. You know . . . she worries . . ."

Miguel nodded. He sat down close to her. Without asking any questions, he took her hand and stayed with her, the quiet interrupted only by her occasional staccato breaths.

"I miss him, too," Miguel whispered, squeezing her hand. "I miss the ranch and Mexico and Abuelita, everything. And I am sorry about what Isabel said to you. I meant nothing by it."

She stared at the dark brown and purple ridges staggered in the distance and let the ripe tears cascade down her cheeks. And this time, Esperanza did not let go of Miguel's hand.

~

They were heading down a steep grade on Highway 99 when Isabel said, "Look!"

Esperanza leaned around the side of the truck. As they rounded a curve, it appeared as if the mountains pulled away from each other, like a curtain opening on a stage, revealing the San Joaquin Valley beyond. Flat and spacious, it spread out like a blanket of patchwork fields. Esperanza could see no end to the plots of yellow, brown, and shades of green. The road finally leveled out on the valley floor, and she gazed back at the mountains from where they'd come. They looked like monstrous lions' paws resting at the edge of the ridge.

A big truck blew its horn and Juan pulled over to let it pass, its bed bulging with cantaloupes. Another truck and another did the same. A caravan of trucks passed them, all piled high with the round melons.

On one side of the highway, acres of grapevines stretched out in soldiered rows and swallowed up the arbors. On the other side, fields and fields of dark green cotton plants became a sea of milk-white puffs. This was not a gently rolling landscape like Aguascalientes. For as far as the eye could travel, the land was unbroken by even a hillock. Esperanza felt dizzy looking at the repeated straight rows of grapes and had to turn her head away.

They finally turned east off the main highway. The truck went slower now and Esperanza could see workers in the fields. People waved and Juan honked the truck horn in return. Then he pulled the truck to the side of the road and pointed to a field that had been cleared of its harvest. Dried, rambling vines covered the acre and leftover melons dotted the ground.

"The field markers are down. We can take as many as we can carry," he called back to them.

Alfonso jumped out, tossed a dozen cantaloupes to Miguel, then stepped up on the running board and slapped the top of the truck for Juan to start again. The melons, warmed by the valley sun, rolled and somersaulted with each bump of the truck.

Two girls walking along the road waved and Juan stopped again. One of them climbed in, a girl about Miguel's age. Her hair was short, black, and curly and her features were sharp and pointed. She leaned back against the side of the truck, her hands behind her head, and she studied Esperanza, her eyes darting at Miguel whenever she could.

"This is Marta," said Isabel. "She lives at another camp where they pick cotton but it is owned by a different company. Her aunt and uncle live at our camp so she stays with them sometimes."

"Where are you from?" asked Marta.

"Aguascalientes. El Rancho de las Rosas," said Esperanza.

"I have never heard of El Rancho de las Rosas. Is that a town?"

"It was the ranch they lived on," said Isabel proudly, her eyes round and shining. "Esperanza's father owned it and thousands of acres of land. She had lots of servants and beautiful dresses and she went to private school, too. Miguel is my cousin and he and his parents worked for them."

"So you're a princess who's come to be a peasant? Where's all your finery?"

Esperanza stared at her and said nothing.

"What's the matter, silver spoon stuck in your mouth?" Her voice was smart and biting.

"A fire destroyed everything. She and her mother have come to work, like the rest of us," said Miguel.

Confused, Isabel added, "Esperanza's nice. Her papa died."

"Well, my father died, too," said Marta. "Before he came to this country, he fought in the Mexican revolution against people like her father who owned all the land."

Esperanza stared back at Marta, unblinking. What had she done to deserve this girl's insults? Through gritted teeth, she said, "You know nothing of my papa. He was a good, kind man who gave much of his property to his servants."

"That might be so," said Marta. "But there were plenty of the rich who did not."

"That was not my papa's fault."

Isabel pointed to one of the fields, trying to change the subject. "Those people are Filipinos," she said. "They live in their own camp. And see over there?" She pointed to a field down the road. "Those people are from Oklahoma. They live in Camp 8. There's a Japanese camp, too. We all live separate and work separate. They don't mix us."

"They don't want us banding together for higher wages or better housing," said Marta. "The owners think if Mexicans have no hot water, that we won't mind as long as we think no one has any. They don't want us talking to the Okies from Oklahoma or anyone else because we might discover that they have hot water. See?"

"Do the Okies have hot water?" asked Miguel.

"Not yet, but if they get it, we will strike."

"Strike?" said Miguel. "You mean you will stop working? Don't you need your job?"

"Of course I need my job, but if all the workers join together and refuse to work, we might all get better conditions."

"Are the conditions so bad?" asked Miguel.

"Some are decent. The place you are going to is one of the better ones. They even have *fiestas*. There's a *jamaica* this Saturday night."

Isabel turned to Esperanza. "You will love the

*jamaicas.* We have them every Saturday night during the summer. There is music and food and dancing. This Saturday is the last for this year because soon it will be too cold."

Esperanza nodded and tried to pay attention to Isabel. Marta and Miguel talked and grinned back and forth. An unfamiliar feeling was creeping up inside of Esperanza. She wanted to toss Marta out of the moving truck and scold Miguel for even talking to her. Hadn't he seen her rudeness?

She brooded as they rode past miles of young tamarisk trees that seemed to be the border of someone's property.

"Beyond those trees is the Mexican camp," said Isabel, "where we live."

Marta smirked at Esperanza and said, "Just so you know. This isn't Mexico. No one will be waiting on you here." Then she gave her a phony smile and said, "*¿Entiendes?* Understand?"

Esperanza stared back at her in silence. The one thing she did understand was that she did not like Marta.

# LAS CEBOLLAS
### O N I O N S

"We're here," said Isabel, as the truck turned into camp and slowed to a crawl. Esperanza stood up and looked over the cab.

They were in a large clearing, surrounded by grape fields. Row upon row of white wooden cabins formed long lines, connected like bunkhouses. Each cabin had one small window and two wooden steps that led to the door. She couldn't help but think that they weren't even as nice as the servants' cabins in Aguascalientes. They reminded Esperanza more of the horse stalls on the ranch than of a place for people to live. A big mountain loomed in the east, framing one side of the valley.

Marta jumped out and ran toward some girls standing together near the cabins. Esperanza could hear them talking in English, the words hard and clipped, as if they were speaking with sticks in their mouths. They all looked at her and laughed. She turned away, thinking that if Isabel could learn English, then maybe someday she could learn it, too.

A line of flatbed trucks pulled into a clearing and *campesinos* hopped down, home from the fields. People called to one another. Children ran to their fathers yelling, "Papi! Papi!" Esperanza felt a deep pang. She watched and wondered how she would fit into this world.

Isabel pointed to a wooden building off to the side. "That's where they have all the toilets."

Esperanza cringed as she tried to imagine having no privacy.

"We're lucky," said Isabel solemnly. "In some camps, we had to go in ditches."

Esperanza looked down at her, swallowed, and nodded, suddenly thankful for something.

A foreman came over and shook hands with Juan and Alfonso and pointed to the cabin in front of the truck. The women got out, took the babies, and helped Miguel with the bags.

Mama and Esperanza walked into the cabin. It

had two small rooms. One half of the front room was the kitchen with a stove, sink, and counter, and a table and chairs. A pile of wood waited near the stove. Across the room was a mattress on the floor. The back room had another mattress big enough for two people and a tiny cot. In between sat a wooden fruit crate, to be used as a night table, its sides touching each bed. Above was another small window.

Mama looked around and then gave Esperanza a weak smile.

"Is this our cabin or Hortensia's and Alfonso's?" asked Esperanza, hoping that hers and Mama's might be better.

"We are all together in this cabin," said Mama.

"Mama, we can't possibly all fit!"

"Esperanza, they will only give one cabin for each man with a family. There is no housing for single women. This is a family camp so we must have a male head of household to live and work here. And that is Alfonso." Mama sank to the bed. Her voice sounded tired. "He has told them we are his cousins and if anyone asks us, we must say it's true. Otherwise we cannot stay. We are next door to Juan and Josefina so we can adjust the sleeping arrangements. Miguel will sleep next door with them and the babies. And Isabel will sleep here with Alfonso, Hortensia, and us."

Miguel came in and set down their valises, then left. Esperanza could hear Alfonso and Hortensia in the next room, talking about the camp office.

Mama got up to unpack and began to sing.

Esperanza felt anger crawling up her throat. "Mama, we are living like horses! How can you sing? How can you be happy? We don't even have a room to call our own."

The talking suddenly stopped in the other room.

Mama gave Esperanza a long, hard look. She calmly walked over and shut the door to the small room.

"Sit down," she said.

Esperanza sat on the tiny cot, its springs screeching.

Mama sat on the bed opposite her, their knees

almost touching. "Esperanza, if we had stayed in Mexico and I had married Tío Luis, we would have had one choice. To be apart and miserable. Here, we have two choices. To be together and miserable or to be together and happy. *Mija*, we have each other and Abuelita will come. How would she want you to behave? I choose to be happy. So which will you choose?"

She knew what Mama wanted to hear. "Happy," she said quietly.

"Do you know how lucky we are, Esperanza? Many people come to this valley and wait months for a job. Juan went to a lot of trouble to make sure we had this cabin waiting for us when we got here. Please be grateful for the favors bestowed upon us." Mama bent over and kissed her, then left the room.

Esperanza laid down on the cot.

A few minutes later, Isabel came in and sat on the bed. "Will you tell me what it was like to be so very rich?"

She looked at Isabel, her eyes anticipating some wonderful story.

Esperanza was quiet for a moment, clinging to one possible thought.

Then she said, "I am still rich, Isabel. We will only be here until Abuelita is well enough to travel. Then she will come with her money and we will buy a big house. A house that Papa would have been proud for us to live in. Maybe we will buy two houses so that Hortensia, Alfonso, and Miguel can live in one and work for us again. And you can visit us, Isabel. You see, this is only temporary. We will not be here for long."

"¿De veras?" asked Isabel.

"Yes, it is the truth," said Esperanza, staring at the ceiling that someone had covered with newspaper and cardboard. "My papa would never have wanted us to live in a place like this." She closed her eyes and heard Isabel tiptoe out of the room and shut the door.

The weariness from the days of travel flooded over her, and her mind wandered from people peeing in ditches, to Marta's rudeness, to the horse stalls at El Rancho de las Rosas.

How could she be happy or grateful when she had never been more miserable in her life?

⁓

When Esperanza opened her eyes again, it was almost light and she heard Mama, Hortensia, and Alfonso talking in the next room. She had slept through dinner and the entire night. She smelled *café* and *chorizo*. The coffee and sausage made her stomach growl and she tried to remember when she had last eaten. Isabel was still asleep in the bed next to hers so Esperanza quietly pulled on a long wrinkled skirt and white blouse. She brushed her hair and went into the other room.

"Good morning," said Mama. "Sit down and eat something. You must be starved."

At the table, Hortensia patted her hand. "You missed going to the foreman's office last night. We signed the papers to live here. We already have work today."

Mama put a plate of *tortillas*, eggs, and sausage in front of her.

"Where did all the food come from?" asked Esperanza.

"Josefina," said Hortensia. "She brought some groceries until we can go to the store this weekend."

"Esperanza," said Mama, "you and Isabel will be watching the babies while the rest of us work. Alfonso and Juan will be picking grapes and Hortensia, Josefina, and I will be packing grapes in the sheds."

"But I want to work with you and Hortensia and Josefina!"

"You're not old enough to work in the sheds," said Mama. "And Isabel is not old enough to watch the babies by herself. If you watch the babies, then Josefina can work and that is one more paying job between us. We must all do our part. You will have a camp job, too, sweeping the wooden platform every afternoon, for which they will deduct a little from our rent each month. Isabel can show you what to do later."

"What's the platform?" Esperanza asked.

"It's the big wooden floor, outside, in the middle of the camp. Juan said they use it for meetings and dances," said Mama.

Esperanza stared at her food. She did not want to be stuck in camp with the children.

"Where's Miguel?" she said.

"He already left for Bakersfield with some other men to look for work at the railroad," said Alfonso.

Isabel came out of the bedroom rubbing her eyes.

"Mi *sobrina*, my niece," said Hortensia, hugging Isabel. "Go say good morning to your mother and father before we all leave for work."

Isabel hugged her and ran next door.

Esperanza studied Mama as she made *un burrito de frijoles* for lunch and wrapped the soft *tortilla* filled with pinto beans in paper. She looked different. Was it the long cotton dress and the big flowered apron tied at her waist? No, it was more than that.

"Mama," said Esperanza. "Your hair!"

Mama's hair ran down her back in a single long

braid, almost touching her waist. Esperanza had never seen Mama wear her hair that way. It was always done up in her beautiful plaited bun, or when she was ready for bed, brushed out and flowing. Mama looked shorter and, somehow, not herself. Esperanza didn't like it.

Mama reached up and stroked the back of her head. She seemed embarrassed. "I . . . I figured out that I can't wear a hat with my hair on top of my head. And this makes more sense, does it not? After all, I am going to work today, not to a *fiesta*." Then she hugged Esperanza. "We must go now. The trucks leave at 6:30 to take us to the sheds. Take good care of the babies and stay with Isabel. She knows the camp."

As the three of them walked out, Esperanza noticed Mama reaching up, hesitantly touching her hair again.

When Esperanza finished eating, she went outside and stood on the front step. Instead of facing another row of cabins, their cabin was in the last row facing the fields. Straight ahead, across a dirt road, were several chinaberry trees and a mulberry tree that provided deep shade over a wooden table. Beyond the row of trees were grape fields, still lush. To the right, across a grassy field, was the main road. A truck piled high with produce drove by, losing a cloud of debris.

After it passed, the sharp smell told her they were onions, the dry outer skins being shredded by the wind. Another truck followed. Again the smell bit into her senses.

It was still early so the air was cool, but the sun was bright and she knew it would be hot soon. The hens pecked and poked around the front steps. They must have been happy to be off the train. Esperanza shooed them out of her way as she turned and walked next door.

The babies were still in their pajamas. Isabel was struggling to feed Lupe her oatmeal while Pepe crawled on the floor. Splotches of his cereal still stuck to his cheeks. As soon as he saw Esperanza, he reached up for her.

"Let's clean them up," said Isabel. "And then I'll show you the camp."

First, Isabel took Esperanza to the platform she

was to sweep and showed her where the brooms were stored. Then they walked through the rows of cabins, each with a baby on her hip. As they passed open doors, Esperanza could already smell the beans and onions that someone had started simmering for dinner. Women were dragging big metal washtubs beneath the shade trees. A group of young boys kicked a ball up and down the dirt road, stirring up dust. A little girl, wearing a man's undershirt as a dress, ran up to Isabel and took her hand.

"This is Silvia. She is my best friend. Next week, we will go to school together."

Silvia switched around and grabbed Esperanza's free hand.

Esperanza looked down at Silvia's dirty hands. Silvia grinned up at her and Esperanza's first thought was to pull her hand away and wash it as soon as possible. Then she remembered Mama's kindness to the peasant girl on the train — and her disappointment in Esperanza. She didn't want Silvia to start crying if she were to pull away. She looked around at the dusty camp and thought that it must be hard to stay clean in such a place. She squeezed Silvia's hand and said, "I have a best friend, too. Her name is Marisol and she lives in Aguascalientes."

Isabel introduced Esperanza to Irene and Melina, two women who were hanging clothes to dry on a long line stretched between the cabins and a tree. Irene had long gray hair tied in a tail. Melina didn't look much older than Miguel and she already had a baby of her own.

"We heard the story of how you came from Aguascalientes," said Melina. "My husband is from there. He used to work for Señor Rodríguez."

Esperanza's face lit up at this news. "He knew my father since he was a boy. Do you think your husband knew Marisol, Señor Rodríguez's daughter?"

Melina laughed. "No, no. I'm sure he didn't. He was *un campesino*, a field servant. He would not know the family."

Esperanza felt awkward and didn't mean to make Melina admit that her husband was a servant. But Melina didn't seem bothered and began recalling other farms her husband had worked on in Aguascalientes.

Isabel pulled on Esperanza's arm. "We need to change the babies."

As they walked back to the cabin, she said, "They are mother and daughter. They come over to talk and crochet with my mother all the time."

"How do they know all about us already?"

Isabel raised her hand and made her fingers tap up and down on her thumb as if a mouth was talking. "Everyone in camp knows each other's business."

⁓

"Do you know how to change a diaper?" asked Esperanza when they got back to the cabin.

"Certainly," said Isabel. "I will change them and you can rinse out the diapers. We need to do some laundry, too."

Esperanza watched as the young girl laid the babies down one at a time, unpinned their diapers, wiped their bottoms clean, and pinned on fresh diapers.

Isabel handed Esperanza the smelly bundles and said, "Take them to the toilets and dump them and I'll fill the washtub."

Esperanza held them at arm's length and almost ran to the toilets. Several more onion trucks passed by, their smell accosting her eyes and nose as much as the diapers. By the time she got back, Isabel had already filled two washtubs with water from an outside pipe and was swirling soap around in one of them. A washboard was propped inside.

Esperanza went to the washtub and hesitated, staring into the water. Bits of onion skins floated on the surface of the soapy water. She held a corner of one of the diapers, lightly dipping it in and out of the water, her hand never getting wet. After a few seconds, she gingerly lifted the diaper from the water. "Now what?" she said.

"Esperanza! You must scrub them! Like this." Isabel walked over, took the diapers, and plunged them into the water up to her elbows. The water quickly became murky. She rubbed the diapers with soap, vigorously scrubbed them back and forth on the washboard, and wrung them out.

Then she transferred them to the next tub, rinsing and wringing again. Isabel shook out the clean diapers and hung them on the line stretched between the chinaberry and mulberry trees. Then she started on the clothes. Esperanza was amazed. She had never washed anything in her life and Isabel, who was only eight years old, made it look so easy.

Puzzled, Isabel looked at Esperanza. "Don't you know how to wash clothes?"

"Well, Hortensia took everything out to the laundry quarters. And the servants, they always . . ." She looked at Isabel and shook her head no.

Isabel's eyes got bigger and she looked worried. "Esperanza, when I go to school next week, you will be here alone with the babies and will have to do the laundry."

Esperanza took a deep breath and said weakly, "I can learn."

"And later today, you must sweep the platform. You . . . you do know how to sweep?"

"Of course," said Esperanza. She had seen

people sweep many times. Many, many times, she assured herself. Besides, she was already too embarrassed about the washing to admit anything else to Isabel.

~

Isabel sat with the babies while Esperanza went to sweep the platform. The camp was quiet and even though it was late in the day, the sun was unrelenting. She retrieved the broom and stepped onto the wooden floor. Dried and brittle onion skins were everywhere.

In her entire life, Esperanza had never held a broom in her hand. But she had seen Hortensia sweep and she tried to visualize the memory. It couldn't possibly be that hard. She put both hands near the middle of the broomstick and moved it back and forth. It swung wildly. The motion seemed awkward and the fine dirt on the wooden planks lifted into a cloud. Onion jackets flew into the air instead of gathering together in a neat pile like Hortensia's. Esperanza's elbows did not know what to do. Neither did her arms. She felt streams of perspiration sliding down her neck. She stopped for a moment and stared at the broom, as if willing it to behave. Determined, she tried again. She hadn't noticed that several trucks were already unloading workers nearby. Then she heard it. First a small tittering and then louder. She turned around. A group of women were laughing at her. And in the middle of the group was Marta, pointing.

"¡La Cenicienta! Cinderella!" she laughed.

Burning with humiliation, Esperanza dropped the broom and ran back to the cabin.

In her room, she sat on the edge of the cot. Her face flushed again at the thought of the ridicule. She was still sitting there, staring at the wall, when Isabel found her.

"I said I could work. I told Mama I could help. But I cannot even wash clothes or sweep a floor. Does the whole camp know?"

Isabel sat down on the bed next to her and patted her back. "Yes."

Esperanza groaned. "I will never be able to show my face." She put her head in her hands until she heard someone else come into the room.

Esperanza looked up to see Miguel, holding a broom and a dustpan. But he wasn't laughing. She looked down and bit her lip so she wouldn't cry in front of him.

He shut the door, then stood in front of her and said, "How would you know how to sweep a floor? The only thing that you ever learned was how to give orders. That is not your fault. Anza, look at me."

She looked up.

"Pay attention," he said, his face serious. "You hold the broom like this. One hand here and the other here."

Esperanza watched.

"Then you push like this. Or pull it toward you like this. Here, you try," he said, holding out the broom.

Slowly, Esperanza got up and took the broom from him. He positioned her hands on the handle.

She tried to copy him but her movements were too big.

"Smaller strokes," said Miguel, coaching. "And sweep all in one direction."

She did as he said.

"Now, when you get all the dirt into a pile, you hold the broom down here, near the bottom, and push the dirt into the pan."

Esperanza collected the dirt.

"See, you can do it." Miguel raised his thick eyebrows and smiled. "Someday, you just might make a very good servant."

Isabel giggled.

Esperanza could not yet find humor in the situation. Somberly she said, "Thank you, Miguel."

He grinned and bowed. "At your service, *mi reina*." But this time, his voice was kind.

She remembered that he had gone to look for work at the railroad. "Did you get a job?"

His smile faded. He put his hands in his pockets and shrugged his shoulders. "It is frustrating. I can fix any engine. But they will only hire Mexi-cans to lay track and dig ditches, not as mechanics. I've decided to work in the fields until I can con-vince someone to give me a chance."

Esperanza nodded.

After he left the room, Isabel said, "He calls you *mi reina!* Will you tell me about your life as a queen?"

Esperanza sat on the mattress and patted the spot next to her. Isabel sat down.

"Isabel, I will tell you all about how I used to live. About parties and private school and beauti-ful dresses. I will even show you the beautiful doll my papa bought me, if you will teach me how to pin diapers, how to wash, and . . ."

Isabel interrupted her. "But that is so easy!"

Esperanza stood up and carefully practiced with the broom. "It is not easy for me."

# LAS ALMENDRAS
## A L M O N D S

"Ay, my neck hurts," said Mama as she massaged the back of her head with her hand.

"It is not my neck. It's my arms that are sore," said Hortensia.

"It is the same for everyone," said Josefina. "When you first start in the sheds, the body refuses to bend, but in time, you will get used to the work."

Everyone had come home that night tired and with various aches and pains. They gathered in one cabin for dinner, so it was crowded and noisy. Josefina warmed a pot of beans and Hortensia made fresh *tortillas*. Juan and Alfonso talked about the fields while Miguel and Isabel played with the babies, making them squeal with laughter. Mama cooked *arroz*, and Esperanza was surprised that Mama knew just how to brown it first in oil with onions and peppers. Esperanza chopped *tomates* for a salad and hoped no one would mention the sweeping. She was glad this day was over. Her bruises had been to her pride.

Isabel took a fresh *tortilla*, sprinkled it with salt, rolled it up like a cigar and waved it at Miguel. "How come you and Tío Alfonso won't let me go behind the cabin with you?"

"Shhh," he said. "It's a surprise."

"Why are you so full of secrets?" asked Esperanza.

But neither Alfonso nor Miguel answered. They simply smiled while they prepared their plates.

They ate dinner, but before they could slice a cantaloupe for dessert, Alfonso and Miguel disappeared, with instructions not to follow them.

"What are they doing?" demanded Isabel.

Hortensia shrugged as if she knew nothing.

Miguel came back just before sunset. "Señora and Esperanza, we have something to show you."

Esperanza looked at Mama. It was obvious Mama was as confused as she was. They all followed Miguel to where Alfonso was waiting.

Behind the cabin was an old oval washtub

with one end cut off. It had been set on its side, forming a little shrine around a plastic statue of Our Lady of Guadalupe. Someone had built a grotto of rocks around the base of the tub. Around it, a large plot of earth had been fenced in by sticks and rope and planted with thorny stems, each with only a few branches.

Isabel gasped. "It's beautiful. Is that our statue?"

Josefina nodded. "But the roses come from far away."

Esperanza searched Miguel's face, her eyes hopeful. "Papa's?"

"Yes, these are your papa's roses," said Miguel, smiling at her.

Alfonso had dug circles of earth around each plant, *casitas*, little houses, that made moats for deep watering. Just like he had done in Aguascalientes.

"But how?" Esperanza remembered the rose garden as a blackened graveyard.

"After the fire, my father and I dug down to the roots. Many were still healthy. We carried the cuttings from Aguascalientes. And that's why we had to keep them wet. We think they will grow. In time, we will see how many bloom."

Esperanza bent closer to look at the stems rooted in mulch. They were leafless and stubby, but lovingly planted. She remembered the night before the fire, when she had last seen the roses and had wanted to ask Hortensia to make rosehip tea. But she'd never had the chance. Now, if they bloomed she could drink the memories of the roses that had known Papa. She looked at Miguel, blinking back tears. "Which one is yours?"

Miguel pointed to one.

"Which one is mine?"

He smiled and pointed to the one that was closest to the cabin wall and already had a makeshift trellis propped against it. "So you can climb," he said.

Mama walked up and down, carefully touching each cutting. She took Alfonso's hands in her own and kissed him on each cheek. Then she went to Miguel and did the same. *"Muchas gracias,"* she said.

Mama looked at Esperanza. "Didn't I tell you that Papa's heart would find us wherever we go?"

～

The next morning, Hortensia put a piece of fabric over the window and sent Alfonso next door with Miguel, Juan, and the babies. Hortensia, Mama, and Josefina brought in the big washtubs and filled them half full with cold water. Then they heated pots of water on the stove and warmed the baths. Esperanza was excited at the idea of getting into a tub. All they had done since they arrived was wash their faces and arms with cold water in the sink. She hadn't had a real bath since she left Aguascalientes. But it was Saturday and tonight was the *jamaica*, so the entire camp was getting cleaned up. Baths were being taken, shirts ironed, and hair washed and crimped.

Hortensia had given Esperanza her baths since she was a baby and they had an established routine. Esperanza stood near the tub with her arms outstretched while Hortensia undressed her. Then she got in the tub and tried not to wiggle while Hortensia washed her. She'd tilt her head back, keeping her eyes closed, while Hortensia rinsed her hair. Finally, she stood up and nodded, which was Hortensia's signal to wrap the towel around her.

Esperanza went to one of the washtubs, put her hands out to her sides, and waited. Josefina looked at Hortensia and raised her eyebrows.

Isabel said, "Esperanza, what are you doing?"

Mama walked over to Esperanza and said softly, "I've been thinking that you are old enough to bathe yourself, don't you think?"

Esperanza quickly dropped her arms and remembered Marta's taunting voice saying, "No one will be waiting on you here."

"Yes, Mama," she said, and for the second time in two days, she felt her face burning as everyone stared at her.

Hortensia came over, put her arm around Esperanza and said, "We are accustomed to doing things a certain way, aren't we, Esperanza? But I guess I am not too old to change. We will help each other. I will unbutton the buttons you cannot reach and you will help Isabel, yes? Josefina, we need more hot water in these tubs. *Ándale,* hurry."

As Hortensia helped her with her blouse, Esperanza whispered, "Thank you."

Isabel and Esperanza went first, bathing in the tubs, then bending their heads over to wash their hair. Mama and Josefina poured cups of water over them to rinse off the soap. The women took turns going back and forth to the stove for hot water. Esperanza liked being with all of them in the tiny room, talking and laughing, and rinsing each other's hair. Josefina and Hortensia talked about all the gossip in the camp. Mama sat in her slip and combed out Isabel's tangles. The women took their turns and when Hortensia needed hot water, Esperanza rushed to get it for her before anyone else could.

Clean and dressed, with still-wet hair, Esperanza and Isabel went outside to the wooden table under the trees. Josefina had given them a burlap bag of almonds that she wanted shelled.

Isabel bent over and brushed her hair in the dry air. "Are you coming to the *jamaica* tonight?" she asked.

Esperanza didn't answer at first. She had not left the cabin since she had made a fool of herself yesterday. "I don't know. Maybe."

"My mama said it is best to get it over with and face people. And that if they tease you, you should just laugh," said Isabel.

"I know," said Esperanza, fluffing her own hair that was already almost dry. She dumped the nuts onto the table and picked up an almond still in its flattened pod. The soft and fuzzy outside hull looked like two hands pressed together, protecting something inside. Esperanza popped it open and found the almond shell. She snapped the edge of the shell and pried it apart, then pulled the meat from its defenses and ate it. "I suppose Marta will be there tonight?"

"Probably," said Isabel. "And all of her friends, too."

"How does she know English?"

"She was born here and her mother, too. They

are citizens," said Isabel, helping shell the almonds. "Her father came from Sonora during the revolution. They have never even been to Mexico. There's lots of kids who live in our camp who have never been to Mexico. My father doesn't like it when Marta comes to our *jamaicas*, though, because she is always talking to people about striking. There was almost a strike during almonds but not enough people agreed to stop working. My mama says that if there had been a strike, we would have had to go into the orchard and shake the trees ourselves for these almonds."

"Then we're lucky. What is your mother making with these nuts?"

"*Flan de almendra*," said Isabel. "She will sell slices at the *jamaica* tonight."

Esperanza's mouth watered. Almond flan was one of her favorite sweets. "Then I've made my decision. I will come."

⁓

The platform was lit up with big lights. Men from the camp, in starched and pressed shirts and cowboy hats, sat in chairs tuning their guitars and violins. Long rows of tables were covered in bright tablecloths where women sold *tamales*, desserts, and the specialty, *Agua de Jamaica*, Hibiscus Flower Water punch made with the red Mexican *jamaica* bloom. There was bingo on wooden tables and a long line of chairs circling the dance area for those who wanted to watch. That's where Mama and Hortensia sat, talking to other women. Esperanza stayed close to them, watching the growing crowd.

"Where do all the people come from?" she asked. The other night, she had heard Juan say that about two hundred people lived in their camp, but there were many more than that now.

"These *fiestas* are popular. People come from other camps," said Josefina. "And from Bakersfield, too."

When the music started, everyone crowded around the platform, clapping and singing. People started dancing in the area around the stage. Children ran everywhere, chasing and hiding. Men held young boys on their shoulders, and women swaddled their infants, all of them swaying to the sounds of the small band.

After a while, Esperanza left Mama and the others and wandered through the noisy crowd, thinking how strange it was that she could be in the middle of so many people and still feel so alone. She saw a group of girls who seemed about her age but they were huddled together. More than anything, she wished Marisol were here.

Isabel found her and pulled on her hand. "Esperanza, come and see."

Esperanza let herself be led through the crowd. Someone from town had brought a litter of kittens. A group of girls were crowded next to the cardboard box, cooing and cradling them. It was clear that Isabel desperately wanted one.

Esperanza whispered to her, "I will go ask your mother." She wove back through the crowd to find Josefina, and when she agreed, Esperanza practically ran back to the spot to tell Isabel. But when she got there, a bigger crowd had gathered and something else was going on.

Marta and some of her friends stood in the bed

of a truck that was parked nearby, each of them holding up one of the tiny kittens.

"This is what we are!" she yelled. "Small, meek animals. And that is how they treat us because we don't speak up. If we don't ask for what is right-fully ours, we will never get it! Is this how we want to live?" She held the kitten by the back of the neck, waving it high in the air. It hung limp in front of the crowd. "With no decent home and at the mercy of those bigger than us, richer than us?"

Isabel trembled, her eyes in a panic. "Will she drop it?"

A man called out, "Maybe all that cat wants to do is feed its family. Maybe it doesn't care what all the other cats are doing."

"Señor, does it not bother you that some of your *compadres* live better than others?" yelled one of Marta's friends. "We are going to strike in two weeks. At the peak of the cotton. For higher wages and better housing!"

"We don't pick cotton on this farm!" yelled an-other man from their camp.

"What does it matter?" yelled Marta. "If we all

132

stop working, if all the Mexicans are *juntos*, to-gether . . ." She made a fist and held it in the air, ". . . then maybe it will help us all!"

He yelled back, "That is a chance we cannot take. We just want to work. That's why we came here. Get out of our camp!"

A cheer rose up around him. People started shoving and Esperanza grabbed Isabel's hand and pulled her aside.

A young man jumped into the truck and started the engine. Marta and the others tossed the kittens into the field. Then they pulled some of their supporters into the back of the truck with them and raised their arms, chanting, "*¡Huelga! ¡Huelga!* Strike! Strike!"

⌒

"Why is she so angry?" asked Esperanza, as she walked back to the cabin a few hours later with Josefina, Isabel, and the babies, leaving the others to stay later. Isabel carried the soft, mewing or-ange kitten in her arms.

"She and her mother move around to find

work, sometimes all over the state," said Josefina. "They work wherever there is something to be harvested. Those camps, the migrant camps, are the worst."

"Like when we were in El Centro?" said Isabel.

"Worse," said Josefina. "Our camp is a company camp and people who work here don't leave. Some live here for many years. That is why we came to this country. To work. To take care of our families. To become citizens. We are lucky because our camp is better than most. There are many of us who don't want to get involved in the strike because we can't afford to lose our jobs, and we are accustomed to how things are in our little community."

"They want to strike for better houses?" asked Esperanza.

"That and more money for those who pick cotton," said Josefina. "They only get seven cents a pound for picking cotton. They want ten cents a pound. It seems like such a small price to pay, but in the past, the growers said no. And now, more people are coming to the valley to look for work, especially from places like Oklahoma, where there is little work, little rain, and little hope. If the Mexicans strike, the big farms will simply hire others. Then what would we do?"

Esperanza wondered what would happen if Mama did not have a job. Would they have to go back to Mexico?

Josefina put the babies to bed. Then she kissed Isabel and Esperanza on their foreheads and sent them next door.

Isabel and Esperanza lay in their beds listening to the music and the bursts of laughter in the background. The kitten, after drinking a bowl of milk, curled up in Isabel's arms. Esperanza tried to imagine conditions that were more shabby than this room that was covered in newspaper to keep out the wind. Could things possibly be worse?

Sleepily, Isabel said, "Did you have parties in Mexico?"

"Yes," whispered Esperanza, keeping her promise to tell Isabel about her old life. "Big parties. Once, my mama hosted a party for one hundred people. The table was set with lace tablecloths, crystal and china, and silver candelabras. The servants cooked for a week . . . " Esperanza continued, reliving the extravagant moments, but was relieved when she knew that Isabel was asleep. For some reason, after hearing about Marta and her family, she felt guilty talking about the richness of her life in Aguascalientes.

Esperanza was still awake when Mama came to bed later. A stream of light from the other room allowed just enough brightness for her to watch Mama unbraid her hair and brush it out.

"Did you like the party?" Mama whispered.

"I miss my friends," said Esperanza.

"I know it is hard. Do you know what I miss? I miss my dresses."

"Mama!" Esperanza said, laughing that Mama would admit such a thing to her.

"Shhh," said Mama. "You will wake Isabel."

"I miss my dresses, too, but we don't seem to need them here."

"That is true. Esperanza, do you know that I am so proud of you? For all that you are learning."

Esperanza snuggled close to her.

Mama continued. "Tomorrow we are going to a church in Bakersfield. After church, we are going to *una tienda*, called Cholita's. Josefina said she sells every type of sweet roll. And Mexican candies."

They were quiet, listening to Isabel's breathing.

"In church, what will you pray for, Esperanza?" asked Mama.

Esperanza smiled. She and Mama had done this many times before they went to sleep.

"I will light a candle for Papa's memory," she said. "I will pray that Miguel will find a job at the railroad. I will ask Our Lady to help me take care of Lupe and Pepe while Isabel is at school. And I will pray for some white coconut candy with a red stripe on the top."

Mama laughed softly.

"But most of all, I will pray that Abuelita will get well. And that she will be able to get her money from Tío Luis's bank. And that she will come soon."

Mama stroked Esperanza's hair.

"What will you pray for, Mama?"

"I will pray for all the things you said, Esperanza, and one more thing besides."

"What's that?"

Mama hugged her. "I will pray for you, Esperanza. That you can be strong. No matter what happens."

# LAS CIRUELAS
### P L U M S

As they walked to the bus stop, Isabel recited a list of concerns to Esperanza, sounding exactly as Josefina and Mama had sounded earlier that morning.

"Put Pepe down for a nap first, and when he falls asleep, put Lupe down. Otherwise they will play and never go to sleep. And Lupe will not eat bananas . . ."

"I know," said Esperanza, repositioning Pepe on her hip.

Isabel handed her Lupe and climbed the steps of the yellow bus. She found a seat and waved from the window. Esperanza wondered who was more worried, she or Isabel?

Esperanza struggled to carry both babies back to the cabin. Thank goodness Isabel had already helped her feed and dress them. She settled them on a blanket on the floor with some tin cups and wood blocks, then put the beans into a big pot on the stove. Hortensia had prepared them earlier with a big onion and a few cloves of garlic and instructed Esperanza to stir them occasionally and let them cook on low heat, adding more water throughout the day. She stirred the beans and watched Lupe and Pepe play. *I wish Abuelita could see me,* she thought. *She would be proud.*

Later, Esperanza looked for something to feed the babies for lunch. A bowl of ripe plums sat on the table. *They should be soft enough to eat,* she thought. She took several, removed the pit and mashed them with a fork. Both babies loved them, reaching for more after each spoonful. Esperanza mashed another three plums and they gobbled every bite. She let them have their fill until they started fussing and reaching for their bottles of milk.

"Enough of lunch," said Esperanza, cleaning their faces and gratefully thinking that it would soon be nap time. She slowly changed their wet diapers, remembering all of Josefina's and Isabel's instructions. She put Pepe down first with his bottle, as directed, and when he fell asleep, she put Lupe next to him. Esperanza lay down, too, wondering why she was so tired, and she dozed.

She woke up to Lupe's whimpering and an atrocious smell. Brown liquid leaked from her diaper. Esperanza picked her up and carried her out of the room so she wouldn't wake Pepe. She changed her into a dry diaper and rolled the soiled one into a ball and put it by the door until she could take it to the toilets. When she put Lupe back down, Pepe was sitting up in bed, in the same condition. She repeated the diaper changing. With both babies clean, she left them in the bed and dashed to the toilets to rinse the diapers. Then she ran back to the cabin.

A different smell greeted her. The beans! She had forgotten to add more water. When she checked the pot, they appeared to be scorched only on the bottom, so she poured in water and stirred them.

The babies cried and never went back to sleep. Both dirtied their diapers again. The wadded pile by the door grew. They must be ill, worried Esperanza. Did they have the flu or was it something they ate? No one else had been sick recently. What had they eaten today? Only their milk and the plums. "The plums," she groaned. They must have been too hard on their stomachs.

What did Hortensia give her when she was a child and was sick? She tried to remember. Rice water! But how did she make it? Esperanza put a pot on the stove and added a cup of rice. She wasn't sure how much water to add but she remembered that when rice didn't come out soft Hortensia always said it needed more water. She added plenty and boiled the rice. Then she poured off the water and let it cool. She sat on the floor with the babies and fed them teaspoons of rice water all afternoon, counting the minutes until Isabel walked through the door.

"What happened?" said Isabel when she arrived and saw the pile of diapers by the door.

"They were sick from the plums," said Esperanza, nodding toward the plate still on the table where she had mashed them.

"Oh, Esperanza, they are too young for raw plums! Everyone knows that plums must be cooked for babies," said Isabel.

"Well, I am not everyone!" yelled Esperanza. She dropped her head and put her hands over her face. Pepe crawled into her lap, making happy gurgling noises.

She looked at Isabel, already sorry for screaming at her. "I didn't mean to yell. It was a long day. I gave them some rice water and they seem to be fine now."

Sounding surprised, Isabel said, "That was exactly the right thing to do!"

Esperanza nodded and let out a long sigh of relief.

That night, no one mentioned the number of rinsed and wrung diapers in the washtub outside the door. Or the beans that were obviously burnt or the pan of rice in the sink. And no one questioned Esperanza when she said that she was exhausted and wanted to go to bed early.

The grapes had to be finished before the first fall rains and had to be picked *rápido*, quickly, so now there were no Saturdays or Sundays in the week, just workdays. The temperature was still over ninety each day, so as soon as Isabel's bus left for school, Esperanza took the babies back to the cabin. She fixed their bottles of milk and let them play while she made the beds. Then she followed Hortensia's instructions for starting dinner before turning to the laundry. She was amazed at the hot, dry air. Often, by the time she had filled the clotheslines that were strung between the trees, she had only minutes to rest before the valley sun dried the clothes crisp and they were ready to fold.

Irene and Melina came over after lunch and Esperanza spread a blanket in the shade. Esperanza liked Melina's company. In some ways, she was a young girl, sometimes playing with Isabel and Silvia, or telling Esperanza gossip as if they were school friends. In other ways, she was grown up, with a nursing baby and a husband, and preferring to crochet with the older women in the evenings.

"Do you crochet?" Melina asked.

"I know a little, but only a few stitches," said Esperanza, remembering Abuelita's blanket of zig-zag rows that she had been too preoccupied to un-pack.

Melina laid her sleeping baby girl on the blan-ket and picked up her needlework. Irene cut apart a fifty-pound flour sack that was printed with tiny flowers, to use as fabric for dresses.

Esperanza tickled Pepe and Lupe and they laughed.

"They adore you," said Melina. "They cried yesterday when I watched them for the few min-utes it took you to sweep the platform."

It was true. Both babies smiled when Esperanza walked into the room, always reaching for her, especially Pepe. Lupe was good-natured and less demanding, but Esperanza learned to watch her closely, as she often tried to wander away. If she turned her back for a minute, Esperanza found herself frantically searching for Lupe.

Esperanza rubbed Lupe's and Pepe's backs,

hoping they would go to sleep soon, but they were restless and wouldn't settle even though they had their bottles. The afternoon sky looked peculiar, tinged with yellow, and there was so much static in the air that the babies' soft hair stuck out.

"Today is the day of the strike," said Melina. "I heard that they were going to walk out this morning."

"Everyone was talking about it last night at the table," said Esperanza. "Alfonso said he is glad that everyone from our camp agreed to continue working. He is proud that we won't strike."

Irene continued working on the flour sack and shaking her head. "So many Mexicans have the revolution still in their blood. I am sympathetic to those who are striking, and I am sympathetic to those of us who want to keep working. We all want the same things. To eat and feed our children."

Esperanza nodded. She had decided that if she and Mama were to get Abuelita here, they could not afford to strike. Not now. Not when they so desperately needed money and a roof over their heads. She worried about what many were saying: If they didn't work, the people from Oklahoma would happily take their jobs. Then what would they do?

A sudden blast of hot wind took the flour sack from Irene's hand and carried it to the fields.

The babies sat up, frightened. Another hot blast hit them, but kept on, and when the edges of the blanket blew up, Lupe reached for Esperanza, whining.

Irene stood up and pointed to the east. The sky was darkening with amber clouds and several brown tumbleweeds bounced toward them.

A roil of brown loomed over the mountains.

"¡Una tormenta de polvo! Dust storm!" said Irene. "Hurry!"

They picked up the babies and ran inside. Irene closed the door and began shutting the windows.

"What's happening?" asked Esperanza.

"A dust storm, like nothing you have seen before," said Melina. "They are awful."

"What about Mama and Hortensia and the others? Alfonso and Miguel . . . they are in the fields."

"They will send trucks for them," said Irene.

Esperanza looked out the window. Thousands of acres of tilled soil were becoming food for *la tormenta* and the sky was turning into a brown swirling fog. Already, she could not see the trees just a few yards away. Then the sound began. Softly at first, like a gentle rain, then harder as the wind blasted the tiny grains of sand against the windows and metal roofs. The dirt showered against the cabin, pitting everything in its path.

"Get away from the window," warned Irene. "The dirt and wind can break the glass."

The finer dust seeped inside and they tried to seal the door by stuffing rags under it. Esperanza couldn't stop thinking about the others. Isabel was at school. The teachers would take care of her. But Mama, Hortensia, and Josefina were in the open shed. She hoped the trucks would bring them soon. And the fields. She could only imagine. Alfonso and Juan and Miguel, could they breathe?

Irene, Melina, and Esperanza sat on the mattress in the front room trying to calm the babies. There was no relief from the heat in the closed room and soon the air was hazy. Irene dampened some towels so they could wipe the babies' and their own faces. When they talked to one another, they tasted the earth.

"How long does it last?" asked Esperanza.

"Sometimes hours," said Irene. "The wind will stop first. And then the dust."

Esperanza heard a meowing from the door. She ran to it and, pushing hard against the wind, opened it a crack. Isabel's kitten, Chiquita, darted in. There was no trace of her orange fur. The cat was powdered brown.

The babies finally fell asleep, drowsy from the heavy air. Irene was right. The wind stopped, but the dust still swirled as if propelled by its own power. Irene and Melina left with Melina's baby, covered beneath a blanket, and rushed to their cabin.

Esperanza waited, nervously pacing the room and worrying about the others.

The school bus came first.

Isabel burst into the cabin, crying, "¡Mi gata, Chiquita!"

Esperanza hugged her. "She is fine but very dirty and hiding under the bed. Are you all right?"

"Yes," said Isabel. "We got to sit in the cafeteria all afternoon and play games with erasers on our heads. But I was worried about Chiquita."

The door opened again and Mama walked into the cabin, her skin covered with an eerie brown chalkiness, and her hair dusted, like the cat's fur.

"Oh, Mama!"

"I am fine, mija," she said, coughing.

Hortensia and Josefina followed and Isabel put her hands on her cheeks in worried surprise. "You . . . you look like raccoons," she said. All of their faces had circles of pink around their eyes where they had squinted against the dust.

"The trucks could not find their way to the shed so all we could do was sit and wait," said

Hortensia. "We hid behind some crates and buried our heads but it did not help much."

Josefina took the babies next door and Mama and Hortensia began washing their arms in the sink, making muddy water. Mama continued to cough.

"What about Alfonso and Juan and Miguel?" asked Esperanza.

"If the trucks could not get to us, they could not get to the fields. We will have to wait," said Hortensia, exchanging a worried look with Mama.

A few hours later, Juan, Alfonso, and Miguel arrived, their clothes stiff and brown, all of them coughing and clearing their throats every few minutes. Their faces were so encrusted with dry dirt that they reminded Esperanza of cracked pottery.

They took turns rinsing in the sink, the pile of brown clothes growing in the basket. When Esperanza looked outside, she could almost see the trees, but the dust was still thick in the air. Mama had a coughing spasm and Hortensia tried to settle her with a glass of water.

When the adults all finally sat down at the

table, Esperanza asked, "What happened with the strike?"

"There was no strike," said Alfonso. "We heard that they were all ready. And that there were hundreds of them. They had their signs. But the storm hit. The cotton is next to the ground and the fields are now buried in dirt and cannot be picked. Tomorrow, they will have no jobs because of an act of God."

"What will we do tomorrow?" asked Esperanza.

"The grapes are higher off the ground," said Alfonso. "The trunks of the vines are covered but the fruit was not affected. The grapes are ready and cannot wait. So *mañana*, we will go back to work."

The next morning, the sky was blue and calm and the dust had left the air. It had settled on the world, covering everything like a suede blanket. Everyone who lived at the camp shook out the powdery soil, went back to work, and came home again, as if nothing had happened.

In a week, they finished cutting the grapes. Then while they finished packing the grapes, they were already talking about preparing for potatoes. The camp routine repeated itself like the regimented rows in the fields. Very little seemed to change, thought Esperanza, except the needs of the earth. And Mama. Mama had changed. Because after the storm, she never stopped coughing.

~

"Mama, you're so pale!" said Esperanza.

Mama carefully walked into the cabin as if she were trying to keep her balance and slumped into a chair in the kitchen.

Hortensia was bustling behind her. "I am going to make her chicken soup with lots of garlic. She had to sit down at work today because she felt faint. But it is no wonder because she is not eating. Look at her, she has lost weight. She has not been herself since that storm and that was a month ago. I think she should go to the doctor."

"Mama, listen to her," pleaded Esperanza.

Mama looked at her weakly, "I am fine. Just tired. I'm not used to the work. And I've told you, doctors are very expensive."

"Irene and Melina are coming over after dinner to crochet," said Esperanza. She thought that would cheer Mama.

"You sit with them," said Mama. "I'm going to lie down until the soup is ready because I have a headache. Then after dinner, I'll go straight to bed and get a good rest. I'll be fine." She coughed, got up, and slowly walked from the room.

Hortensia looked at Esperanza, shaking her head.

A few hours later, Esperanza stood over Mama. "Your soup is ready, Mama."

But she didn't move. "Mama, dinner," said Esperanza, reaching for her arm and gently shaking her. Mama's arm was burning, her cheeks were flushed red, and she wasn't waking.

Esperanza felt panic squeezing her and she screamed, "Hortensia!"

~

The doctor came. He was American, light and blond, but he spoke perfect Spanish.

"He looks very young to be a doctor," said Hortensia.

"He has come to the camp before and people trust him," said Irene. "And there are not many doctors who will come out here."

Alfonso, Juan, and Miguel sat on the front steps, waiting. Isabel sat on the mattress, her eyes worried. Esperanza could not sit still. She paced near the bedroom door, trying to hear what was going on inside.

When the doctor finally came out, he looked grim. He walked over to the table where all the women sat. Esperanza followed him.

The doctor signaled for the men and waited until everyone was inside.

"She has Valley Fever."

"What does that mean?" asked Esperanza.

"It's a disease of the lungs that is caused by dust spores. Sometimes, when people move to this area and aren't used to the air here, the dust spores get into their lungs and cause an infection."

"But we were all in the dust storm," said Alfonso.

"When you live in this valley, everyone inhales the dust spores at one time or another. Most of the time, the body can overcome the infection. Some people will have no symptoms at all. Some will feel like they have the flu for a few days. And others, for whatever reason, cannot fight the infection and get very sick."

"How sick?" asked Hortensia.

Esperanza sat down.

"She may have a fever on and off for weeks but you must try to keep it down. She will cough and have headaches and joint aches. She might get a rash."

"Can we catch it from her? The babies?" asked Josefina.

"No," said the doctor. "It isn't contagious. And the babies and young children have probably had a mild form of it already, without you even knowing. Once the body fights off the infection, it doesn't get it again. For those who live here most of their lives, they are naturally immunized. It is hardest on adults who move here and are not accustomed to the agricultural dust."

"How long until she is well?" asked Esperanza.

The doctor's face looked tired. He ran his hand through his short blond hair.

"There are some medicines she can take, but even then, if she survives, it might take six months for her to get her full strength back."

Esperanza felt Alfonso behind her, putting his hands on her shoulders. She felt the blood drain from her face. She wanted to tell the doctor that she could not lose Mama, too. That she had already lost Papa and that Abuelita was too far away. Her voice strangled with fear. All she could do was whisper the doctor's uncertain words, "If she survives."

# LAS PAPAS
### P O T A T O E S

Esperanza almost never left Mama's side. She sponged her with cool water and fed her teaspoons of broth throughout the day. Miguel offered to take over the sweeping job for her, but Esperanza wouldn't let him. Irene and Melina arrived each morning, to check on Mama and to take the babies. Alfonso and Juan put up extra layers of newspaper and cardboard in the bedroom to keep out the November chill and Isabel drew pictures to hang on the walls because she did not think the newspaper looked pretty enough for Mama.

The doctor came back a few weeks later with more medicine. "She is not getting worse," he said, shaking his head. "But she is not getting better, either."

Mama drifted in and out of fitful sleep and sometimes she called out for Abuelita. Esperanza could barely sit still and often paced around the small room.

One morning, Mama said weakly, "Esperanza . . ."

Esperanza ran to her and took her hand.

"Abuelita's blanket . . ." she whispered.

Esperanza pulled her valise from under the bed. She had not opened it since before the dust storm and saw that the fine brown powder had even found its way deep inside. As it had found its way into Mama's lungs.

She lifted out the crocheting that Abuelita had started the night Papa died. It seemed like a lifetime ago. Had it only been a few months? She stretched out the zigzag rows. They reached from one side of Mama's bed to the other, but were only a few hands wide, looking more like a long scarf than the beginnings of a blanket. Esperanza could see Abuelita's hairs woven in, so that all her love and good wishes would go with them forever. She held the crocheting to her face and could still smell the smoke from the fire. And the faintest scent of peppermint.

Esperanza looked at Mama, breathing uneasily, her eyes closed. It was clear she needed Abuelita.

They both needed her. But what was Esperanza to do? She picked up Mama's limp hand and kissed it. Then she handed the strip of zigzag rows to Mama, who clutched it to her chest.

What had Abuelita told her when she'd given her the bundle of crocheting? And then she remembered. She had said, "Finish this for me, Esperanza . . . and promise me you'll take care of Mama."

After Mama fell asleep, Esperanza picked up the needlework and began where Abuelita had left off. Ten stitches up to the top of the mountain. Add one stitch. Nine stitches down to the bottom of the valley, skip one. Her fingers were more nimble now and her stitches were more even. The mountains and valleys in the blanket were easy. But as soon as she reached a mountain, she was headed back down into a valley again. Would she ever escape this valley she was living in? This valley of Mama being sick?

What else had Abuelita said? After she had lived many mountains and valleys they would be together again. She bent over her work, intent, and when her hair fell into her lap, she picked it up and wove it into the blanket. She cried when she thought of the wishes that would go into the blanket forever.

Because she was wishing that Mama would not die.

The blanket grew longer. And Mama grew more pale. Women in the camp brought her extra skeins of yarn and Esperanza didn't care that they didn't match. Each night when she went to bed, she put the growing blanket back over Mama, covering her in hopeful color.

Lately, it seemed Esperanza could not interest Mama in anything. "Please, Mama," she begged, "you must eat more soup. Please Mama, you must drink more juice. Mama, let me comb your hair. It will make you feel better."

But Mama was listless and Esperanza often found her weeping in silence. It was as if after all her hard work in getting them there, her strong and determined mother had given up.

The fields frosted over and Mama began to have trouble breathing. The doctor came again, with worse news. "She should be in the hospital. She's very weak but more than that, she is depressed and needs nursing around the clock if she is to get stronger. It is a county hospital so you would not have to pay, except for doctor bills and medicines."

Esperanza shook her head no. "The hospital is where people go to die." She began to cry.

Isabel ran to her crying, too.

Hortensia walked over and folded them both into her arms. "No, no, she is going to the hospital to get better."

Hortensia wrapped Mama in blankets and Alfonso drove them to Kern General Hospital in Bakersfield. The nurses would let Esperanza stay with Mama only a few minutes. And when Esperanza kissed her good-bye, Mama didn't say a word, but just shut her eyes and drifted off to sleep.

Riding home in the truck that evening, Esperanza stared straight into the alley of light made from the truck's headlamps, feeling as if she were in a trance. "Hortensia, what did the doctor mean when he said that Mama was depressed?"

"In only a few months, she has lost her husband, her home, her money. And she is separated from her mother. It is a lot of strain on her body to cope with so many emotions in such a short time. Sometimes sadness and worry can make a person sicker. Your mother was very strong through your father's death and her journey here. For you. But when she got sick, everything became too much for her. Think of how helpless she must feel." Hortensia took out her handkerchief and blew her nose, too upset to continue.

Esperanza felt like she had failed Mama in some way and wanted to make it up to her. Mama had been strong for her. Now it was her turn to be strong for Mama. She must show her that she didn't need to worry anymore. But how? "Abuelita. I must write to Abuelita."

Hortensia shook her head. "I'm sure your uncles are still watching everything that goes in and out of the convent and probably the post office, too.

But maybe we can find someone going to Aguascalientes who can carry a letter."

"I have to do something," said Esperanza, holding back tears. Hortensia put her arm around Esperanza. "Don't worry," she said. "The doctors and nurses know what she needs and we will take care of one another."

Esperanza didn't say what she really thought, that what Mama really needed was Abuelita. Because if sadness was making Mama sicker, then maybe some happiness would make her better. She just had to figure out a way to get her here.

When she got back to camp, she went behind the cabin to pray in front of the washtub grotto. Someone had knit a shawl and draped it over Our Lady's shoulders and the sweetness of the gesture made Esperanza cry. "Please," she said through her tears. "I promised Abuelita I would take care of Mama. Show me how I can help her."

⌣

The next day, Esperanza pulled a heavy shawl around her shoulders and waited for Miguel to come home from the fields. She paced in the area where the trucks unloaded, and wrapped the wool tighter against the early winter cold. She had been thinking all day about what to do. Ever since Mama had first become sick over a month ago, they had no money coming in. The doctor's bills and medicines had used up most of what they'd saved. Now there were more bills. Alfonso and Hortensia offered to help but they had done so much already and they did not have much to spare. Besides, she could not accept their charity forever.

Abuelita's ankle was probably healed by now, but if she hadn't been able to get her money out of Tío Luis's bank, then she would have no money with which to travel. If Esperanza could somehow get money to Abuelita, then maybe she could come sooner.

When Miguel jumped off one of the trucks, she called to him.

"What have I done to deserve this honor, *mi reina?*" he said, smiling and walking toward her.

"Please, Miguel, no teasing. I need help. I need to work so I can bring Abuelita to Mama."

He was quiet and Esperanza could tell he was thinking. "But what could you do? And who would take care of the babies?"

"I could work in the fields or in the sheds and Melina and Irene have already offered to watch Pepe and Lupe."

"It's only men in the fields right now, and you're not old enough to work in the sheds."

"I am tall. I'll wear my hair up. They won't know."

"The problem is that it's the wrong time of year. They aren't packing anything right now. Not until asparagus in the spring. My mother and Josefina are going to cut potato eyes for the next three weeks. Maybe you can go with them?"

"But it is just three weeks," said Esperanza. "I need more work than that!"

"Anza, if you're good at cutting potato eyes, they will hire you to tie grapes. If you are good at tying grapes, they will hire you for asparagus. That's how it works. If you're good at one thing, then they hire you for another."

She nodded. "Can you tell me one more thing, Miguel?"

"*Claro*. Certainly."

"What are potato eyes?"

~

Esperanza huddled with Josefina, Hortensia, and a small group of women waiting for the morning truck to take them to the sheds. A thick tule ground fog that hugged the earth settled in the valley, surrounding them, as if they stood within a deep gray cloud. There was no wind, only silence and penetrating cold.

Esperanza bundled in all the clothing that she could put on, old wool pants, a sweater, a ragged jacket, a wool cap, and thick gloves over thin gloves, all borrowed from friends in the camp. Hortensia had shown her how to heat a brick in the oven and bundle it in newspaper, and she hugged it to her body to keep warm as they rode on the truck.

Since the driver could only see a few yards

ahead, the truck rumbled slowly on the dirt roads. They passed miles of naked grapevines, stripped of their harvest and bereft of their leaves. Fading into the mist, the brown and twisted trunks looked frigid and lonely.

The truck stopped at the big packing shed. It was really one long building with different open-air sections, as long as six train cars. The railroad tracks ran along one side, and docks for trucks ran along the other. Esperanza had heard Mama and the others talk about the sheds. How they were busy with people; women standing at long tables, packing the fruit; trucks coming and going with their loads fresh from the fields; and workers stocking the train cars that would later be hooked to a locomotive to take the fruit all over the United States.

But cutting potato eyes was different. Since nothing was being packed, there wasn't the usual activity. Only twenty or so women gathered in the cavernous shed, sitting in a circle on upturned crates, protected from the wind by only a few stacks of empty boxes.

The Mexican supervisor took their names.

With all the clothing they were wearing, he barely looked at their faces. Josefina had told Esperanza that if she was a good worker, the bosses would not concern themselves with her age, so she knew she would have to work hard.

Esperanza copied everything that Hortensia and Josefina did. When the women put the hot bricks between their feet to keep them warm while they worked, so did she. When they took off their outer gloves and worked in thin cotton ones, she did the same. Everyone had a metal bin sitting behind them. The field-workers brought cold potatoes and filled up their bins. Hortensia took a potato and then, with a sharp knife, she cut it into chunks around the dimples. She tapped her knife on one of the dimples. "That is an eye," she whispered to Esperanza. "Leave two eyes in every piece so there will be two chances for it to take root." Then she dropped the chunks into a burlap sack. When the sack was full, the field-workers took it away.

"Where do they take them?" she asked Hortensia.

"To the fields. They plant the eye pieces and then the potatoes grow."

Esperanza picked up a knife. Now she knew where potatoes came from.

The women began chatting. Some knew each other from camp. And one of them was Marta's aunt.

"Is there any more talk of striking?" asked Josefina.

"Things are quiet now, but they are still organizing," said Marta's aunt. "There is talk of striking in the spring when it is time to pick. We are afraid there will be problems. If they refuse to work, they will lose their cabins in the migrant camps. And then where will they live? Or worse, they will all be sent back to Mexico."

"How can they send all of them back?" asked Hortensia.

"Repatriation," said Marta's aunt. "*La Migra* — the immigration authorities — round up people who cause problems and check their papers. If they are not in order, or if they do not happen to have their papers with them, the immigration officials send them back to Mexico. We have heard that they have sent people whose families have lived here for generations, those who are citizens and have never even been to Mexico."

Esperanza remembered the train at the border and the people being herded on to it. She had been thankful for the papers that Abuelita's sisters had arranged.

Marta's aunt said, "There is also some talk about harming Mexicans who continue to work."

The other women sitting around the circle pretended to concentrate on their potatoes, but Esperanza noticed worried glances and raised eyebrows.

Then Hortensia cleared her throat and said, "Are you saying that if we continue to work during the spring, your niece and her friends might harm us?"

"We are praying that does not happen. My husband says we will not join them. We have too many mouths to feed. And he has told Marta she cannot stay with us. We can't risk being asked to leave the camp or losing our jobs because of our niece."

Heads nodded in sympathy and the circle was silent, except for the sounds of the knives cutting the crisp potatoes.

"Is anyone going to Mexico for *La Navidad?*" asked another woman, wisely changing the subject. Esperanza kept cutting the potato eyes but listened carefully, hoping someone would be going to Aguascalientes for Christmas. But no one seemed to be traveling anywhere near there.

A worker refilled Esperanza's metal bin with another load of cold potatoes. The rumbling noise brought her thoughts back to what Marta's aunt had said. If it was true that the strikers would threaten people who kept working, they might try and stop her, too. Esperanza thought of Mama in the hospital and Abuelita in Mexico and how much depended on her being able to work. If she was lucky enough to have a job in the spring, no one was going to get in her way.

A few nights before Christmas, Esperanza helped Isabel make a yarn doll for Silvia while the others went to a camp meeting. Ever since Esperanza had taught Isabel how to make the dolls, it seemed there was a new one born each day, and *monas* of every color now sat in a line on their pillows.

"Silvia will be so surprised," said Isabel. "She has never had a doll before."

"We'll make some clothes for it, too," said Esperanza.

"What was Christmas like at El Rancho de las Rosas?" Isabel never tired of Esperanza's stories about her previous life.

Esperanza stared up at the ceiling, searching her memories. "Mama decorated with Advent wreaths and candles. Papa set up the nativity on a bed of moss in the front hall. And Hortensia cooked for days. There were *empanadas* filled with meat and sweet raisin *tamales*. You would have loved how Abuelita decorated her gifts. She used dried grapevines and flowers, instead of ribbons. On Christmas Eve, the house was always filled with laughter and people calling out, '*Feliz Navidad.*' Later, we went to the *catedral* and sat with hundreds of people and held candles during midnight mass. Then we came home in the middle of the night, still smelling of incense from the church, and drank warm *atole de chocolate*, and opened our gifts."

Isabel sucked in her breath and gushed, "What kind of gifts?"

"I . . . I can't remember," said Esperanza, braiding the yarn doll's legs. "All I remember is being happy." Then she looked around the room as if seeing it for the first time. One of the table legs was uneven and had to be propped by a piece of wood so it wouldn't wiggle. The walls were patched and peeling. The floor was wood plank and splintery and no matter how much she swept, it never looked clean. The dishes were chipped and the blankets frayed and no amount of beating could remove their musty smell. Her other life seemed like a story she had read in a book a long time ago, *un cuento de hadas*, a fairy tale. She could see the illustrations in her mind: the Sierra Madre, El Rancho de las Rosas, and a carefree young girl running through the vineyard. But now, sitting in this cabin, the story seemed as if it were about some other girl, someone Esperanza didn't know anymore.

"What do you want for Christmas this year?" asked Isabel.

"I want Mama to get well. I want more work. And . . ." She stared at her hands and took a deep breath. After three weeks of potato eyes, they were dried and cracked from the starch that had soaked through her gloves. ". . . I want soft hands. What do you want, Isabel?"

Isabel looked at her with her big doe eyes and said, "That's easy. I want anything!"

Esperanza nodded and smiled. Admiring the completed doll, she handed it to Isabel, whose eyes, as usual, were excited.

They went to bed, Isabel in her cot, and Esperanza in the bed that she and Mama had slept in. She turned toward the wall, yearning for the holidays of her past, and repeated what was becoming a nightly ritual of silent tears. She didn't think anyone ever knew that she cried herself to sleep, until she felt Isabel patting her back.

"Esperanza, don't cry again. We will sleep with you, if you want."

We? She turned toward Isabel, who was holding the family of yarn dolls.

Esperanza couldn't help but smile and lift the covers. Isabel slid in beside her, arranging the dolls between them.

Esperanza stared into the dark. Isabel had nothing, but she also had everything. Esperanza wanted what she had. She wanted so few worries that something as simple as a yarn doll would make her happy.

⁓

On Christmas Day Esperanza walked up the front steps of the hospital while Alfonso waited in the truck. A couple passed her carrying gifts wrapped in shiny paper. A woman hurried by, carrying a poinsettia plant and wearing a beautiful red wool coat with a rhinestone Christmas tree pinned to the lapel. Esperanza's eyes riveted on the coat and the jewelry. She wished she could give Mama a warm red coat and a pin that sparkled. She thought of the gift she had in her pocket. It was nothing more than a small smooth stone that she had found in the fields while weeding potatoes.

The doctor had moved Mama to a ward for people with long-term illnesses. There were only four other people on the floor and the patients were spread out, their occupied beds scattered among the rows of bare mattresses in the long room. Mama slept and didn't wake even to say hello. Nevertheless, Esperanza sat next to her, crocheted a few rows on the blanket and told Mama about the sheds and Isabel and the strikers. She told her that Lupe and Pepe could almost walk now. And that Miguel thought that Papa's roses showed signs of growth.

Mama didn't wake to say good-bye either. Esperanza tucked the blanket around her, hoping that the color from the blanket would slowly seep into Mama's cheeks.

She put the stone on the night table and kissed Mama good-bye.

"Don't worry. I will take care of everything. I will be *la patrona* for the family now."

# LOS AGUACATES
### A V O C A D O S

Esperanza's breath made smoky vapors in front of her face as she waited for the truck to take her to tie grapevines. She shifted from foot to foot and clapped her gloved hands together and wondered what was so new about the New Year. It already seemed old, with the same routines. She worked during the week. She helped Hortensia cook dinner in the late afternoons. In the evenings she helped Josefina with the babies and Isabel with her homework. She went to see Mama on Saturdays and Sundays.

She huddled in the field near a smudge pot to keep warm and mentally counted the money she would need to bring Abuelita here. Every other week, with the small amounts she saved, she bought a money order from the market and put it in her valise. She figured that if she kept working until peaches, she would have enough for

Abuelita's travel. Her problem then would be how to reach Abuelita.

The men went down the rows first, pruning the thick grapevines and leaving a few long branches or "canes" on each trunk. She followed, along with others, and tied the canes on the taut wire that was stretched post to post. She ached from the cold and had to keep moving all day long to stay warm.

That night, as she soaked her hands in warm water, she realized that she no longer recognized them as her own. Cut and scarred, swollen and stiff, they looked like the hands of a very old man.

"Are you sure this will work?" asked Esperanza, as she watched Hortensia cut a ripe avocado in half.

"Of course," said Hortensia, removing the big pit and leaving a hole in the heart of the fruit. She scooped out the pulp, mashed it on a plate, and added some glycerine. "You have seen me make this for your mother many times. We are lucky to have the avocados this time of year. Some friends of Josefina brought them from Los Angeles."

Hortensia rubbed the avocado mixture into Esperanza's hands. "You must keep it on for twenty minutes so your hands will soak up the oils."

Esperanza looked at her hands covered in the greasy green lotion and remembered when Mama used to sit like this, after a long day of gardening or after horseback rides with Papa through the dry mesquite grasslands. When she was a little girl, she had laughed at Mama's hands covered in what looked like *guacamole*. But she had loved for her to rinse them because afterward, Esperanza would take Mama's hands and put the palms on her own face so she could feel their suppleness and breathe in the fresh smell.

Esperanza was surprised at the simple things she missed about Mama. She missed her way of walking into a room, graceful and regal. She missed watching her hands crocheting, her fingers moving nimbly. And most of all, she longed for the sound of Mama's strong and assured laughter.

She put her hands under the faucet, rinsed off the avocado, and patted them dry. They felt better, but still looked red and weathered. She took another avocado, cut it in half, swung the knife into the pit and pulled it from the flesh. She repeated Hortensia's recipe and as she sat for the second time with her hands smothered, she realized that it wouldn't matter how much avocado and glycerine she put on them, they would never look like the hands of a wealthy woman from El Rancho de las Rosas. Because they were the hands of a poor *campesina*.

~

It was at the end of grape-tying when the doctor stopped Esperanza and Miguel in the hallway of the hospital before they could reach Mama's room.

"I asked the nurses to alert me when they saw you coming. I'm sorry to tell you that your mother has pneumonia."

"How can that be?" said Esperanza, her hands beginning to shake as she stared at the doctor. "I thought she was getting better."

"This disease, Valley Fever, makes the body

tired and susceptible to other infections. We are treating her with medications. She is weak. I know this is hard for you, but we'd like to ask that she have no visitors for at least a month, maybe longer. We can't take a chance that she will contract another infection from any outside germs that might be brought into the hospital."

"Can I see her, just for a few moments?"

The doctor hesitated, then nodded, and walked away.

Esperanza hurried to Mama's bed and Miguel followed. Esperanza couldn't imagine not seeing her for so many weeks.

"Mama," said Esperanza.

Mama slowly opened her eyes and gave Esperanza the smallest smile. She was thin and frail. Her hair was strewn and bedraggled. And her face was so white that it seemed to fade into the sheets, as if she would sink into the bed and disappear forever. Mama looked like a ghost of herself.

"The doctor said I can't come to visit for a while."

Mama nodded, her eyelids slowly falling back down, as if it had been a burden to keep them up.

Esperanza felt Miguel's hand on her shoulder.

"Anza, we should go," he said.

But Esperanza would not move. She wanted to do something for Mama to help make her better. She noticed the brush and hairpins on the bedside table.

She carefully rolled Mama on her side and gathered all of her hair together. She brushed it and plaited it into a long braid. Wrapping it around Mama's head, she gently pinned it into place. Then she helped Mama lie on her back, her hair now framing her face against the white linens, like a braided halo. Like she used to wear it, in Aguascalientes.

Esperanza bent down close to Mama's ear. "Don't worry, Mama. Remember, I will take care of everything. I am working and I can pay the bills. I love you."

Mama said softly, "I love you, too." And as Esperanza turned to leave, she heard Mama whisper, "No matter what happens."

"You need to get away from the camp, Esperanza," said Hortensia as she handed her the grocery list and asked her to go to the market with Miguel. "It is the first of spring and it's beautiful outside."

"I thought you and Josefina always looked forward to marketing on Saturday," said Esperanza.

"We do, but today we are helping Melina and Irene make *enchiladas*. Could you go for us?"

Esperanza knew they were trying to keep her occupied. Mama had been in the hospital for three months and Esperanza hadn't been allowed to visit for several weeks. Since then, Esperanza hadn't been acting like herself. She went through the motions of living. She was polite enough, answering everyone's questions with the simplest answers, but she was tormented by Mama's absence. Papa, Abuelita, Mama. Who would be next?

She crawled into bed as early as possible each night, curled her body into a tight ball, and didn't move until morning.

She knew Josefina and Hortensia were worried about her. She nodded to Hortensia, took the list, and went to find Miguel.

"Be sure you tell Miguel to go to Mr. Yakota's market!" Hortensia called after her.

Hortensia had been right about the weather. The fog and grayness had gone. The valley air was crisp and clean from recent rains. They drove along fields of tall, feathery asparagus plants that she would soon be packing. Citrus groves displayed their leftover fruit like decorations on Christmas trees. And even though it was still cool, there was an expectancy that Esperanza could smell, a rich loamy odor that promised spring.

"Miguel, why must we always drive so far to shop at the Japanese market when there are other stores closer to Arvin?"

"Some of the other market owners aren't as kind to Mexicans as Mr. Yakota," said Miguel. "He stocks many of the things we need and he treats us like people."

"What do you mean?"

"Esperanza, people here think that all Mexicans are alike. They think that we are all uneducated, dirty, poor, and unskilled. It does not occur to them that many have been trained in professions in Mexico."

Esperanza looked down at her clothes. She wore a shirtwaist dress that used to be Mama's and before that, someone else's. Over the dress was a man's sweater with several buttons missing, which was also too big. She leaned up and looked in the mirror. Her face was tanned from the weeks in the fields, and she had taken to wearing her hair in a long braid like Hortensia's because Mama had been right — it was more practical that way. "Miguel, how could anyone look at me and think I was uneducated?"

He smiled at her joke. "The fact remains, Esperanza, that you, for instance, have a better education than most people's children in this country. But no one is likely to recognize that or take the time to learn it. Americans see us as one big, brown group who are good for only manual labor. At this market, no one stares at us or treats us like outsiders or calls us 'dirty greasers.' My father says that Mr. Yakota is a very smart businessman. He is getting rich on other people's bad manners."

Miguel's explanation was familiar. Esperanza's contact with Americans outside the camp had been limited to the doctor and the nurses at the hospital, but she had heard stories from others about how they were treated. There were special sections at the movie theater for Negroes and Mexicans. In town, parents did not want their children going to the same schools with Mexicans. Living away from town in the company camp had its advantages, she decided. The children all went to school together: white, Mexican, Japanese, Chinese, Filipino. It didn't seem to matter to anyone because they were all poor. Sometimes she felt as if she lived in a cocoon, protected from much of the indignation.

Miguel pulled the truck into the parking lot at the market. "I'll meet you. I'm going to talk about railroad jobs with those men gathered on the corner."

Esperanza went inside. Mr. Yakota was from

Tokyo and the store had all sorts of Japanese cooking ingredients like seaweed and ginger, and a fresh fish counter with fish that still had their heads. But there were Mexican products, too, like *masa de harina* for *tamales*, *chiles* for *salsa*, and big bags of dried beans for *frijoles*. There was even cow's intestine in the meat case for *menudo*. And other specialties, like *chorizo* and pigs' feet. Esperanza's favorite part of the store was the ceiling that was crowded with a peculiar combination of Japanese paper lanterns and *piñatas* shaped like stars and donkeys.

There was a small tissue donkey that Esperanza had not noticed before. It was like the one Mama had bought her a few years ago. Esperanza had thought it so cute that she had refused to break it, even though it had been filled with sweets. Instead, she had hung it in her room above her bed.

A clerk walked by and impulsively, she pointed to the miniature *piñata*. "*Por favor,*" she said. "Please."

She bought the other things she needed, including another money order. That was one more benefit of Mr. Yakota's market: She could buy money orders there.

She was waiting in the truck when Miguel came back.

"Another money order? What do you do with them all?" asked Miguel.

"I save them in my valise. They are for such small amounts but together, they'll be enough to someday bring Abuelita here."

"And the *piñata*? It's not anyone's birthday."

"I bought it for Mama. I'm going to ask the nurses to put it near her bed, so she'll know that I'm thinking of her. We can stop by the hospital on the way back. Will you cut a hole in the top for me so I can put the caramels inside? The nurses can eat them."

He took out his pocket knife and made an opening in the *piñata*. While Miguel drove, Esperanza began feeding in the caramels.

Not far down the main road, they approached an almond grove, the trees flush with gray-green leaves and white blossoms. Esperanza noticed a girl and a woman walking hand in hand, each with a grocery bag in her other arm. She couldn't help but think what a nice scene it made, with the two women framed against so many spring blossoms.

Esperanza recognized one of them. "I think that is Marta."

Miguel stopped the truck, then slowly backed up. "We should give her a ride."

Esperanza reluctantly nodded, remembering the last time they'd given her a lift, but she opened the door.

"Esperanza and Miguel, *que buena suerte*. What good luck," said Marta. "This is my mother, Ada. Thanks for the ride."

Marta's mother had the same short, curly black hair but hers was sprinkled with gray.

Miguel got out and put all the groceries in the truck bed so they could sit in the front.

Ada said, "I heard about your mother and I've been praying for her."

Esperanza was surprised and touched. "Thank you, I'm grateful."

"Are you coming to our camp?" asked Miguel.

"No," said Marta. "As you probably know, I'm not welcome there. We're going a mile or so up the road to the strikers' farm. We were tossed out of the migrant workers' camp and were told either to go back to work or leave. So we left. We aren't going to work under those disgusting conditions and for those pitiful wages."

Ada was quiet and nodded when Marta talked about the strike. Esperanza felt a twinge of envy when she noticed that Marta never let go of her mother's hand.

"There are hundreds of us together at this farm, but thousands around the county and more people join our cause each day. You are new here, but in time, you'll understand what we're trying to change. Turn left," she said, pointing to a dirt road rutted with tire marks.

Miguel turned down the path bordered in cotton fields. Finally, they reached several acres of land surrounded by chain-link fencing and barbed wire, its single opening guarded by several men wearing armbands.

"*Aquí.* Right here," said Ada.

"What are the guards for?" asked Esperanza.

"They're for protection," said Marta. "The farmer who owns the land is sympathetic to us but a lot of people don't like the strikers causing trouble. We've had threats. The men take turns at the entrance."

Miguel pulled the truck to the side of the road and stopped.

There were only ten wooden toilet stalls for hundreds of people and Esperanza could smell the effects from the truck. Some people lived in tents but others had only burlap bags stretched between poles. Some were living in their cars or old trucks. Mattresses were on the ground, where people and dogs rested. A goat was tied to a tree. There was a long pipe that lay on top of the ground and a line of water spigots sticking up from it. Near each spigot were pots and pans and campfire rings, the makings of outdoor kitchens. In an irrigation ditch, women were washing clothes, and children were bathing at the same time. Clotheslines ran everywhere. It was a great jumble of humanity and confusion.

Esperanza could not stop looking. She felt hypnotized by the squalor but Marta and her mother didn't seem the least bit embarrassed.

"Home, sweet home," said Marta.

They all climbed out of the truck, but before Marta and Ada could retrieve their groceries, a *campesino* family coming from the opposite direction approached them. The children were dirty and skinny and the mother held an infant, who was crying.

"Do you have food so that I can feed my family?" said the father. "We were thrown out of our camp because I was striking. My family has not eaten in two days. There are too many people coming into the valley each day who will work for pennies. Yesterday I worked all day and made less than fifty cents and I cannot buy food for one day with that. I was hoping that here, with others who have been through the same . . ."

"You are welcome here," said Ada.

Esperanza reached into the truck bed and opened the large bag of beans. "Hand me your hat, Señor."

The man handed over his large sun hat and she filled it with the dried beans, then gave it back to him.

"*Gracias, gracias,*" he said.

Esperanza looked at the two older children, their eyes watery and vacant. She lifted the *piñata* and held it out to them. They said nothing but hurried toward her, took it, and ran back to their family.

Marta looked at her. "Are you sure you aren't already on our side?"

Esperanza shook her head. "They were hungry, that's all. Even if I believed in what you are doing, I must take care of my mother."

Ada put her hand on Esperanza's arm and smiled. "We all do what we have to do. Your mother would be proud of you."

Miguel handed them their bags, and they walked toward the farmer's field. Before they reached the gate, Marta suddenly turned and said, "I shouldn't be telling you this, but the strikers are more organized than they appear. In a few weeks, during asparagus, things are going to happen all over the county. We're going to shut down every-thing, the fields, the sheds, the railroad. If you have not joined us by then, be very careful." Then she hurried to catch up with her mother.

As Miguel and Esperanza rode back to Arvin, neither of them said a word for many miles. Marta's threat and the guilt of having a job weighed heavily on Esperanza's mind. "Do you think they are right?" she asked.

"I don't know," said Miguel. "What the man said is true. I have heard that there will be ten times the people here looking for jobs in the next few months, from Oklahoma, Arkansas, Texas, and other places, too. And that they are poor people like us, who need to feed their families, too. If so many come and are willing to work for pennies, what will happen to us? But until then, with so many joining the strikes, I might be able to get a job at the railroad."

Esperanza's mind wrestled with Miguel's words. For him, the strike was an opportunity to work at the job he loved and to make it in this country, but for her, it was a threat to her finances, Abuelita's arrival, and Mama's recuperation. Then there was the matter of her own safety. She thought of Mama and Abuelita, and she knew there was only one thing for her to do.

~

Esperanza studied her hands a few nights later as she walked toward the cabin and hoped Hortensia had a few more avocados. It was later than usual. She had been weeding asparagus in a far field so she had been on the last truck. When she arrived at the cabin, everyone was crowded around the small table. There were fresh *tortillas* on a plate and Hortensia was stirring a pan of *machaca*, scrambled eggs with shredded meat, onions, and peppers. It was Miguel's favorite but they usually ate it for breakfast.

"What is the occasion?" asked Esperanza.

"I got a job in the machine shop at the railroad."

"Oh, Miguel! That's good news!"

"So many railroad workers have joined the strikers. I know it might be temporary but if I do a good job, maybe they will keep me."

"That is right," said Alfonso. "You do good work. They will see it. They will keep you."

Esperanza sat down and listened to Miguel tell the others about the job, but she wasn't hearing his words. She was seeing his eyes, dancing like Papa's when he used to talk about the land. She watched Miguel's animated face, thinking that at last, his dream was coming true.

# LOS ESPÁRRAGOS
## ASPARAGUS

Marta was right. The strikers were more organized than ever. They handed out flyers in front of every store. They painted the sides of old barns with their slogans and held big meetings at the farm. For those who continued to work, there were still jobs, but Esperanza could hear the tightness and worry in her neighbors' voices. She worried, too, about what would happen if she didn't have a job.

Asparagus would be a long season, sometimes up to ten weeks. But it had to be picked before the high temperatures touched the valley in June. The strikers knew that if they could slow down the workers, it would affect the growers, so when the tender stalks were ready, the strikers were ready, too.

Esperanza got on the flatbed truck with Hortensia and Josefina for the first day of packing. The company had sent a man with a gun to ride on the truck with them, for protection they said, but the gun frightened Esperanza.

When they arrived at the sheds, a crowd of women erupted into shouting and booing. They carried signs that said, "¡Huelga! Strike!" Among them were Marta and her friends. And they were yelling.

"Help us feed our children!"

"We must all join together if we are all to eat!"

"Save your countrymen from starving!"

When Esperanza saw their menacing faces, she wanted to run back to the safety of the camp, do laundry, clean diapers, anything but this. She wanted to tell them that her mother was sick. That she had to pay the bills. She wanted to explain to them about Abuelita and how she had to find a way to get some money to her so she could travel. Then maybe they'd understand why she needed her job. She wanted to tell them that she did not want anyone's children to starve. But she knew it would not matter. The strikers only listened if you agreed with them.

She reached for Hortensia's hand and pulled

her close. Josefina marched toward the shed, looking straight ahead. Hortensia and Esperanza stayed close behind, never letting go of each other.

One of the women from their camp called out. "We make less money packing asparagus than you do when you pick cotton. Leave us alone. Our children are hungry, too."

When the guard wasn't looking, one of the strikers picked up a rock and threw it at the woman, barely missing her head, and the workers all hurried toward the shed.

The strikers stayed near the road, but Esperanza's heart was still beating wildly as she and the women took their places to pack the asparagus. All day, as she sorted and bundled the delicate spears, she heard their chanting and their threats.

That night at dinner Alfonso and Juan told how they had the same problems in the fields. Strikers waited for them and they had to cross picket lines to get to work. Once in the fields, they were safe, protected by guards the company had sent. But the lugs of asparagus that were sent back to the sheds had to be taken across the picket lines and the strikers often slipped surprises beneath the harvest.

The strike continued for days. One afternoon, as Josefina took a handful of asparagus from a crate, a large rat jumped out at her. A few days later, Esperanza heard a terrible scream from one of the women and several writhing gopher snakes slithered out of a crate. They found razor blades and shards of glass in the field bins and the women, usually efficient and quick to unpack the asparagus, slowed down and were hesitant to grab the vegetables from their boxes. When several of them heard a rattling from beneath a pile of stalks, the supervisors took the entire crate out to the yard, dumped it, and found an angry rattlesnake inside.

"It was a miracle that no one was bitten by that snake," said Hortensia that night at dinner. They were all gathered in one cabin, eating *caldo de albóndigas*, meatball soup.

"Did you see it?" asked Isabel.

"Yes," said Esperanza. "We all saw it. It was

frightening but the supervisor cut its head off with the hoe."

Isabel cringed.

"Can't they do anything to the strikers?" asked Hortensia.

"It's a free country," said Miguel. "Besides, the strikers are careful. As long as they stay near the road and the guards don't actually see them do anything aggressive, then no, there's not much anyone can do. It's the same at the railroad. I pass the picket lines every day, and listen to the yelling and the insults."

"It's the yelling all day long that bothers me," said Hortensia.

"Remember, do not respond to them," said Alfonso. "Things will get better."

"Papa," said Miguel. "Things will get worse. Have you seen the cars and trucks coming through the pass in the mountains? Every day, more and more people. Some of them say they will pick cotton for five and six cents a pound, and will pick produce for less. People cannot survive on such low wages."

"Where will it end?" said Josefina. "Everyone will starve if people work for less and less money."

"That is the strikers' point," said Esperanza.

No one said anything. Forks clinked on the plates. Pepe, who was sitting in Esperanza's lap, dropped a meatball on the floor.

"Are we going to starve?" asked Isabel.

"No, *mija*," said Josefina. "How could anyone starve here with so much food around us?"

Esperanza had grown so accustomed to the strikers' chanting while she packed asparagus that the moment it stopped, she looked up from her work as if something was wrong.

"Hortensia, do you hear that?"

"What?"

"The silence. There is no more yelling."

The other women on the line looked at each other. They couldn't see the street from where they stood so they moved to the other end of the shed, cautiously looking out to where the strikers usually stood.

In the distance, a caravan of gray buses and police cars headed fast toward the shed, dust flying in their wakes.

"Immigration!" said Josefina. "It is a sweep."

The picket signs lay on the ground, discarded, and like a mass of marbles that had already been hit, the strikers scattered into the fields and toward the boxcars on the tracks, anywhere they could hide. The buses and cars screeched to a stop and immigration officials and police carrying clubs jumped out and ran after them.

The women in the packing shed huddled together, protected by the company's guard.

"What about us?" said Esperanza, her eyes riveted on the guards who caught the strikers and shoved them back toward the buses. They would surely come into the shed next with so many Mexicans working here. Her fingers desperately clenched Hortensia's arm. "I cannot leave Mama."

Hortensia heard the panic in her voice. "No, no, Esperanza. They are not here for us. The growers need the workers. That is why the company guards us."

Several immigration officials accompanied by police began searching the platform, turning over boxes and dumping out field bins. Hortensia was right. They ignored the workers in their stained aprons, their hands still holding the green asparagus. Finding no strikers on the dock, they jumped back down and hurried to where a crowd was being loaded onto the buses.

"¡Americana! ¡Americana!" yelled one woman and she began to unfold some papers. One of the officials took the papers from her hand and tore them into pieces. "Get on the bus," he ordered.

"What will they do with them?" asked Esperanza.

"They will take them to Los Angeles, and put them on the train to El Paso, Texas, and then to Mexico," said Josefina.

"But some of them are citizens," said Esperanza.

"It doesn't matter. They are causing problems for the government. They are talking about forming a farm workers' union and the government and the growers don't like that."

"What about their families? How will they know?"

"Word gets out. It is sad. They leave the buses parked at the station until late at night with those they captured on board. Families don't want to be separated from their loved ones and usually go with them. That is the idea. They call it a voluntary deportation. But it is not much of a choice."

Two immigration officials positioned themselves in front of the shed. The others left on the buses. Esperanza and the other women watched the despondent faces in the windows disappear.

Slowly, the women reassembled on the line and began to pack again. It had all lasted only a few minutes.

"What happens now?" asked Esperanza.

"*La Migra* will keep their eyes open for any strikers that might be back," said Josefina, nodding toward the two men stationed nearby. "And we go back to work and feel thankful it is not us on that bus."

Esperanza took a deep breath and went back to her spot. She was relieved, but still imagined the anguish of the strikers. Troubled thoughts stayed in her mind. Something seemed very wrong about sending people away from their own "free country" because they had spoken their minds.

She noticed she needed more bands to wrap around the asparagus bundles and walked to the back of the dock to get them. Within a maze of tall crates, she searched for the thick rubber bands. Some of the boxes had been tossed over by the immigration officials and as she bent down to set one straight, she sucked in her breath, startled by what was in front of her.

Marta was huddled in a corner, holding her finger to her lips, her eyes begging for help. She whispered, "Please, Esperanza. Don't tell. I can't get caught. I must take care of my mother."

Esperanza stood frozen for a moment, remembering Marta's meanness that first day in the truck. If she helped her and someone found out, Esperanza would be on the next bus herself. She couldn't risk it and started to say no. But then she thought about Marta and her mother holding hands, and couldn't imagine them being separated from each other. And besides, they were both citizens. They had every right to be here.

She turned around and headed back to where the others were working. No one paid any attention to her. They were all busy talking about the sweep. She picked up a bundle of asparagus, several burlap sacks from a stack, and a dirty apron that someone had left on a hook. She quietly wandered back to Marta's hiding place. "*La Migra* is still out front," she said in a hushed voice. "They will probably leave in an hour when the shed closes." She handed the apron and the asparagus to Marta. "When you leave, put on the apron and carry the asparagus so you'll look like a worker, just in case anyone stops you."

"*Gracias,*" whispered Marta. "I'm sorry I misjudged you."

"Shhh," said Esperanza, repositioning the crates and draping the burlap sacks across their tops so Marta couldn't be seen.

"Esperanza," called Josefina, "where are you? We need the rubber bands."

Esperanza stuck her head around the corner and

saw Josefina with her hands on her hips, waiting. "Coming," she called. She grabbed a bundle of bands and went back to work as if nothing had happened.

~

Esperanza lay in bed that night and listened to the others in the front room talk about the sweeps and the deportations.

"They went to every major grower and put hundreds of strikers on the buses," said Juan.

"Some say they did it to create more jobs for those coming from the east," said Josefina. "We are lucky the company needs us right now. If they didn't, we could be next."

"We have been loyal to the company and the company will be loyal to us!" said Alfonso.

"I'm just glad it's over," said Hortensia.

"It is not over," said Miguel. "In time, they will be back, especially if they have families here. They will reorganize and they will be stronger. There will come a time when we will have to decide all over again whether to join them or not."

Esperanza tried to go to sleep but the day spun in her mind. She was glad she had kept working and thankful that her camp had voted not to strike, but she knew that under different circumstances, it could have been her on that bus. And then what would Mama have done? Her thoughts jumped back and forth. Some of those people did not deserve their fate today. How was it that the United States could send people to Mexico who had never even lived there?

She couldn't stop thinking about Marta. It didn't matter if Esperanza agreed with her cause or not. No one should have to be separated from her family. Had Marta made her way back to the strikers' farm without getting caught? Had she found her mother?

For some reason, Esperanza had to know.

❦

The next morning, she begged Miguel to drive by the farm.

The field was still surrounded by the chain-link fence, but no one was protecting the entrance this time. All the evidence of people she had seen before was there, but not one person was to be seen. Laundry waved on the clothesline. Plates with rice and beans sat on crates and swarmed with busy flies. Shoes were lined up in front of tents, as if waiting for someone to step into them. The breeze picked up loose newspapers and floated them across the field. It was quiet and desolate, except for the goat still tied to the tree, bleating for freedom.

"Immigration has been here, too," said Miguel. He got out of the truck, walked over to the tree, and untied the goat.

Esperanza looked out over the field that used to be crawling with people who thought they could change things — who were trying to get the attention of the growers and the government to make conditions better for themselves and for her, too.

More than anything, Esperanza hoped that Marta and her mother were together, but now there would be no way for her to find out. Maybe Marta's aunt would hear, eventually.

Something colorful caught her eye. Dangling from a tree branch were the remnants of the little donkey *piñata* that she had given the children, its tissue streamers fluttering in the breeze. It had been beaten with a stick, its insides torn out.

# LOS DURAZNOS
### PEACHES

Now, along with her prayers for Abuelita and Mama, Esperanza prayed for Marta and her mother at the washtub grotto. Papa's roses, although still short and squat, had promising tight buds, but they weren't the only flowers there. She often found that someone had put a posy of sweet alyssum in front of the statue, or a single iris, or had draped a honeysuckle vine over the top of the tub. Lately, she had seen Isabel there every evening after dinner, kneeling on the hard ground.

"Isabel, are you saying a novena?" asked Esperanza when she found her at the statue, yet again one night. "It seems you have been praying for at least nine days."

Isabel got up from her dedication and looked up at Esperanza. "I might be Queen of the May. In two weeks, on May Day, there is a festival at my school and a dance around a pole with colored ribbons. The teacher will choose the best girl student in the third grade to be queen. And right now, I am the only one who has straight As."

"Then it might be you!" said Esperanza.

"My friends told me that it is usually one of the English speakers that is chosen. The ones who wear nicer dresses. So I'm going to pray every day."

Esperanza thought about all the beautiful dresses she had outgrown in Mexico. How she wished she could have passed them on to Isabel. Esperanza began to worry that she would be disappointed. "Well, even if you are not the queen, you will still be a beautiful dancer, right?"

"Oh, but Esperanza. I want so much to be the queen! I want to be *la reina*, like you."

She laughed. "But regardless, you will always be our queen."

Esperanza left her there, devoutly praying, and went into the cabin.

"Has a Mexican girl ever been chosen Queen of the May?" she asked Josefina.

Josefina's face took on a disappointed look and

she silently shook her head no. "I have asked. They always find a way to choose a blonde, blue-eyed queen."

"But that's not right," said Esperanza. "Especially if it is based on grades."

"There is always a reason. That is the way it is," said Josefina. "Melina told me that last year the Japanese girl had the best marks in the third grade and still they did not choose her."

"Then what is the point of basing it on marks?" asked Esperanza, knowing there was no answer to her question. Her heart already ached for Isabel.

~

A week later Esperanza put yet another bundle of asparagus on the table after work. The tall and feathery asparagus plants seemed to be as unrelenting as Isabel's desire to be queen. The workers picked the spears from the fields and a few days later, the same fields had to be picked again because new shoots were already showing their heads. And Isabel talked of nothing else, except the possibility of wearing the winner's crown of flowers on her head.

"I hate asparagus," said Isabel, barely looking up from her homework.

"During grapes, you hate grapes. During potatoes, you hate potatoes. And during asparagus, you hate asparagus. I suppose that during peaches, you will hate peaches."

Isabel laughed. "No, I love peaches."

Hortensia stirred a pot of beans and Esperanza took off the stained apron she wore in the sheds and put on another. She began measuring the flour to make *tortillas*. In a few minutes, she was patting the fresh dough that left her hands looking as if she wore white gloves.

"My teacher will choose the Queen of the May this week," said Isabel. Her entire body wiggled with excitement.

"Yes, you have told us," said Esperanza, teasing her. "Do you have anything new to tell us?"

"They are making a new camp for people from Oklahoma," said Isabel.

Esperanza looked at Hortensia. "Is that true?"

Hortensia nodded. "They announced it at the camp meeting. The owner of the farm bought some army barracks from an old military camp and is moving them onto the property not too far from here."

"They get inside toilets and hot water! And a swimming pool!" said Isabel. "Our teacher told us all about it. And we will all be able to swim in it."

"One day a week," said Hortensia, looking at Esperanza. "The Mexicans can only swim on Friday afternoons, before they clean the pool on Saturday mornings."

Esperanza pounded the dough a little too hard. "Do they think we are dirtier than the others?"

Hortensia did not answer but turned to the stove to cook a *tortilla* on the flat black *comal* over the flame. She looked at Esperanza and held her finger to her mouth, signaling her not to discuss too much in front of Isabel.

Miguel walked in, kissed his mother, then

picked up a plate and a fresh *tortilla* and went to the pot of beans. His clothes were covered in mud that had dried gray.

"How did you get so dirty?" asked Hortensia.

Miguel sat down at the table. "A group of men showed up from Oklahoma. They said they would work for half the money and the railroad hired all of them." He looked into his plate and shook his head. "Some of them have never even worked on a motor before. My boss said that he didn't need me. That they were going to train the new men. He said I could dig ditches or lay tracks if I wanted."

Esperanza stared at him, her floured hands in midair. "What did you do?"

"Can you not tell from my clothes? I dug ditches." His voice was sharp but he continued eating, as if nothing were wrong.

"Miguel, how could you agree to such a thing?" said Esperanza.

Miguel raised his voice. "What would you have me do instead? I could have walked out. But I would have no pay for today. Those men from

Oklahoma have families, too. We must all work at something or we will all starve."

A temper Esperanza did not recognize raged to the surface. Then, like the irrigation pipes in the fields when the water is first turned on, her anger burst forth. "Why didn't your boss tell the others to dig the ditches?!" She looked at the dough she was holding in her hand and threw it at the wall. It stuck for an instant, and then slowly slid down the wall, leaving a darkened trail.

Isabel's serious eyes darted from Miguel to Esperanza to Hortensia. "Are we going to starve?"

"No!" they all answered at the same time.

Esperanza's eyes were on fire. She stamped out of the cabin, slamming the door, and walked past the mulberry and the chinaberry trees to the vineyard. She hurried down a row, then cut over to another.

"Esperanza!"

She heard Miguel's voice in the distance but she didn't answer. When she got to the end of one row, she moved up to another.

"Anza!"

She could hear him running down the rows, catching up with her.

She kept her eyes on the tamarisk trees in the far distance and walked faster.

Miguel eventually caught her arm and pulled her around. "What is the matter with you?"

"Is this the better life that you left Mexico for? Is it? Nothing is right here! Isabel will certainly not be queen no matter how badly she wants it because she is Mexican. You cannot work on engines because you are Mexican. We have gone to work through angry crowds of our own people who threw rocks at us, and I'm afraid they might have been right! They send people back to Mexico even if they don't belong there, just for speaking up. We live in a horse stall. And none of this bothers you? Have you heard that they are building a new camp for Okies, with a swimming pool? The Mexicans can only swim in it on the afternoon before they clean it! Have you heard they will be given inside toilets and hot water? Why is that,

Miguel? Is it because they are the fairest in the land? Tell me! Is this life really better than being a servant in Mexico?"

Miguel looked out over the grapes where the sun set low on the horizon, casting long shadows in the vineyard. He turned back to her.

"In Mexico, I was a second-class citizen. I stood on the other side of the river, remember? And I would have stayed that way my entire life. At least here, I have a chance, however small, to become more than what I was. You, obviously, can never understand this because you have never lived without hope."

She clenched her fists and closed her eyes tight in frustration. "Miguel, do you not understand? You are still a second-class citizen because you act like one, letting them take advantage of you like that. Why don't you go to your boss and confront him? Why don't you speak up for yourself and your talents?"

"You are beginning to sound like the strikers, Esperanza," said Miguel coldly. "There is more than one way to get what you want in this country. Maybe I must be more determined than others to succeed, but I know that it will happen. *Aguántate tantito y la fruta caerá en tu mano.*"

The words stopped her as if someone had slapped her face. Papa's words: Wait a little while and the fruit will fall into your hand. But she was tired of waiting. She was tired of Mama being sick and Abuelita being far away and Papa being dead. As she thought about Papa, tears sprang from her eyes and she suddenly felt weary, as if she had been clinging to a rope but didn't have the strength to hold on any longer. She sobbed with her eyes closed and imagined she was falling, with the wind whooshing past her and nothing but darkness below.

"Anza."

*Could I fall all the way back to Mexico if I never opened my eyes again?*

She felt Miguel's hand on her arm and opened her eyes.

"Anza, everything will work out," he said.

Esperanza backed away from him and shook her head, "How do you know these things, Miguel?

Do you have some prophecy that I do not? I have lost everything. Every single thing and all the things that I was meant to be. See these perfect rows, Miguel? They are like what my life would have been. These rows know where they are going. Straight ahead. Now my life is like the zigzag in the blanket on Mama's bed. I need to get Abuelita here, but I cannot even send her my pitiful savings for fear my uncles will find out and keep her there forever. I pay Mama's medical bills but next month there will be more. I can't stand your blind hope. I don't want to hear your optimism about this land of possibility when I see no proof!"

"As bad as things are, we have to keep trying."

"But it does no good! Look at yourself. Are you standing on the other side of the river? No! You are still a peasant!"

With eyes as hard as green plums, Miguel stared at her and his face contorted into a disgusted grimace. "And you still think you are a queen."

The next morning, Miguel was gone.

He had told his father he was going to northern California to look for work on the railroad. Hortensia was confused and worried that he would leave so suddenly, but Alfonso reassured her. "He is determined. And he is seventeen now. He can take care of himself."

Esperanza was too ashamed to tell anyone what was said in the vineyard and she secretly knew Miguel's leaving was her fault. When she saw Hortensia's anxiety, Esperanza felt the heavy responsibility for his safety.

She went to Papa's roses and when she saw the first bloom, her heart ached because she wished she could run and tell Miguel. *Please, Our Lady,* she prayed, *don't let anything happen to him or I will never be able to forgive myself for the things I said.*

~

Esperanza kept her mind off Miguel by working hard and concentrating on Isabel. When Esperanza saw a lug of early peaches come into the shed, she set aside a bag to bring home to her. She just had to have them, especially today.

As she walked down the row of cabins after work, she could see Isabel in the distance, waiting for her. Isabel sat up straight, primly, with her small hands folded in her lap, her eyes searching the row. When she saw Esperanza, she jumped up and ran toward her. As she got closer, Esperanza could see the tear streaks on her cheeks.

Isabel threw her arms around Esperanza's waist. "I did not win Queen of the May!" she said, sobbing into the folds of her skirt. "I had the best grades but the teacher said she chose on more than just grades."

Esperanza wanted desperately to make it up to her. She picked her up and held her. "I'm sorry, Isabel. I'm so sorry that they did not choose you." She put her down and took her hand and they walked back to the cabin.

"Have you told the others? Your mother?"

"No," she sniffed. "They are not home yet. I was supposed to go to Irene and Melina's but I wanted to wait for you."

Esperanza took her into the cabin and sat on the bed next to her. "Isabel, it does not matter who won. Yes, you would have made a beautiful queen but that would have lasted for only one day. A day goes by fast, Isabel. And then it is over."

Esperanza bent down, pulled her valise from under the bed, and opened it. The only thing left inside was the porcelain doll. She had shown it to Isabel many times, telling her the story of how Papa had given it to her. Although a little dusty, the doll still looked lovely, its eyes hopeful like Isabel's usually were.

"I want you to have something that will last more than one day," said Esperanza. She lifted the doll from the valise and handed it to Isabel. "To keep as your own."

Isabel's eyes widened. "Oh n . . . no, Esperanza," she said, her voice still shaky and her face wet with tears. "Your papa gave her to you."

Esperanza stroked Isabel's hair. "Do you think my papa would want her buried inside a valise all this time with no one playing with her? Look at her. She must be lonely. She is even getting dusty!

And look at me. I am much too old for dolls. People would make fun of me if I carried her around, and you know how I hate it when people laugh at me. Isabel, you would be doing me and my papa a favor if you would love her."

"Really?" said Isabel.

"Yes," said Esperanza. "And I think that you should take her to school to show all your friends, don't you agree? I'm sure none of them, not even the Queen of the May, has ever owned anything as beautiful."

Isabel cradled the doll in her arms, her tears drying on her face. "Esperanza, I prayed and prayed about being Queen of the May."

"Our Lady knew that being queen would not last, but that the doll would be yours for a long time."

Isabel nodded, a small smile beginning. "What will your mama say?"

Esperanza hugged her, "I have a meeting with the doctor this week so if he lets me, I will ask her. But I think that Mama would be very proud that she belongs to you." Then, grinning, she held out the bag of peaches. "I hate asparagus, too."

~

Esperanza and Hortensia waited in the doctor's office. Hortensia sat and tapped her foot, and Esperanza paced, looking at the diplomas on the wall.

Finally, the door swung open and the doctor walked in, then scooted behind his desk and sat down.

"Esperanza, I have good news," he said. "Your mother's health has improved and she'll be well enough to leave the hospital in a week. She is still a little depressed but I think she needs to be around all of you. Please remember, though, that once she goes home, she will have to rest to build up her strength. There is still a chance of a relapse."

Esperanza started laughing and crying at the same time. Mama was coming home! For the first time in the five months since Mama had entered the hospital, Esperanza's heart felt lighter.

The doctor smiled. "She has been asking for her crochet needles and yarn. You can see her now for a few minutes if you like."

Esperanza ran down the hospital halls with Hortensia behind her to Mama's bedside, where they found her sitting up in bed. Esperanza flung her arms around her neck. "Mama!"

Mama hugged her then held her at arm's length and studied her. "Oh, Esperanza, how you've grown. You look so mature."

Mama still looked thin but not so weak. Esperanza felt her forehead and there was no fever.

Mama laughed at her. It wasn't a strong laugh but Esperanza loved the sound.

Hortensia pronounced that her color was good and promised to purchase more yarn so that it would be waiting when she came home. "You would not believe your daughter, Ramona. She always gets called to work in the sheds, she cooks now, and takes care of the babies as well as their own mother."

Mama reached up, pulled Esperanza to her chest, and hugged her. "I am so proud of you."

Esperanza hugged Mama back. When the visiting hour was over, she hated to leave but kissed Mama and said her good-byes, promising to tell her everything as soon as she came home.

~

All week they prepared for Mama's homecoming. Hortensia and Josefina scrubbed the little cabin until it was almost antiseptic. Esperanza washed all the blankets and propped the pillows in the bed. Juan and Alfonso cushioned a chair and several crates under the shade trees so that Mama could recline outside during the hot afternoons.

On Saturday, as soon as Esperanza helped Mama from the truck, she wanted a quick tour of Papa's roses and she got weepy when she saw the blooms. Visitors came all afternoon, but Hortensia would only let people stay a few minutes, then she shooed them away for fear Mama wouldn't get her rest.

That night, Isabel showed Mama the doll and how she was taking care of it and Mama told her that she thought Isabel and the doll belonged together. When it was time for bed, Esperanza carefully lay down next to Mama, hoping she wouldn't disturb her, but Mama moved closer and put her arms around Esperanza, and held her tightly.

"Mama, Miguel is gone," she whispered.

"I know, *mija*. Hortensia told me."

"But Mama, it was my fault. I got angry and told him he was still a peasant and then he left."

"It could not have been all your fault. I'm sure he knows you didn't mean it. He'll come back soon. He couldn't be away from his family for long."

They were quiet.

"Mama, we've been away from Abuelita for almost a year," said Esperanza.

"I know," said Mama quietly. "It does not seem possible."

"But I've saved money. We can bring her soon. Do you want to see how much?" Before Mama could answer, Esperanza turned on the light, checking to make sure she hadn't woken Isabel. She tiptoed to the closet and took out her valise. She grinned at Mama, knowing how proud she would be of all the money orders. She opened the bag and her mouth dropped open. She couldn't believe what she saw. She tipped the valise upside down and shook it hard.

It was empty. The money orders were gone.

# LAS UVAS
### GRAPES

**M**iguel was the only one who could have taken the money orders. No one doubted that. Alfonso apologized to Esperanza, but Mama graciously said that Miguel must have needed the money to get to northern California. Alfonso promised the money would be paid back, one way or another, and Esperanza knew it would be, but she was angry with Miguel. How dare he go into her valise and take what was not his. And after all her hard work.

Mama seemed to get a little stronger every day, although she still took many naps. Hortensia was happy that she was eating well, and every day Esperanza brought home just-picked fruit to tempt her.

A few weeks later, Esperanza stood on the shed dock in the morning and marveled at the peaches, plums, and nectarines that poured into the shed.

"How will we ever sort them all?" she asked.

Josefina laughed. "One piece at a time. It gets done."

They started with the small white clingstone peaches and then the larger yellow Elbertas. Mama loved the white peaches so Esperanza set aside a bag for her. Then after lunch, they sorted the Flaming Gold nectarines. Later that afternoon they would still have to sort a few bushels of plums.

Esperanza loved the elephant-heart plums. Mottled green on the outside and bloodred on the inside, they were tangy and sweet at the same time. She stood in the midsummer sun during her lunch break and ate one, bent over so the juice wouldn't run down her chin.

Josefina called to her. "*Mira*," she said. "Look. There's Alfonso. What is he doing here?"

Alfonso was talking to one of the supervisors. He had never left the fields in the middle of the day and come to the sheds.

"Something must be wrong," said Esperanza.

"Maybe it is the babies?" said Josefina and she hurried toward him.

Esperanza could see them talking and slowly began walking toward them, leaving the line of women and the stacks of lugs and plums. She tried to read from Josefina's expressions whether something was wrong. Then Josefina turned to look at her.

Esperanza felt the blood drain from her face and she suddenly knew why Alfonso was here. It had to be Mama. The doctor had said she could have a relapse. Something must have happened to her. Esperanza suddenly felt weak but she kept walking. "Is it Mama?"

"No, no. I didn't mean to alarm you, Esperanza, but I need you to come with me. Hortensia is in the truck."

"But it's so early."

"It's okay, I talked to the supervisor."

She followed him to the truck. Hortensia was waiting inside. "We got a message from Miguel," she said. "We are to meet him at the bus station in Bakersfield at three o'clock. He said he is coming from Los Angeles and that we should bring you. That's all we know."

"But why would he want me to come?" asked Esperanza.

"I can only hope that it's to apologize for his actions," said Hortensia.

It was over a hundred degrees. Hot wind whipped inside the cab. Esperanza felt the perspiration sliding down her skin beneath her dress. It felt strange to be riding to town on a workday, breaking her routine in the sheds. She kept thinking of all the elephant hearts that the others would have to pack shorthanded.

Hortensia squeezed her hand. "I can't wait to see him," she said.

Esperanza offered a tight smile.

They arrived at the bus station and sat on a bench in front. The clerks all spoke to one another in English, their hard, sharp words meaning nothing to Esperanza. It always startled her when she heard English and she hated not knowing what people were saying. Someday she would learn it. She strained to hear each announcement that was made, finally hearing the words she was waiting for, "Los Angeles."

A silver bus turned the corner and pulled into the bay in front of the station. Esperanza searched through the passengers seated on the bus but couldn't see Miguel. She and Hortensia and Alfonso stood up and watched everyone get off. And then, finally, there was Miguel standing in the doorway of the bus. He looked tired and rumpled but when he saw his parents, he jumped from the steps, grabbing his mother and hugging her, then his father, clapping him on the back.

He looked at Esperanza and smiled. "I have brought you proof that things will get better," he said.

She looked at him, trying to be angry. She didn't want him to think she was glad to see him. "Did you bring back what you have stolen?"

"No, but I brought you something better."

Then he turned to help the last passenger from the bus, a small, older woman trying to get down the steep steps. The sun, reflecting off the shiny bus, glinted in Esperanza's eyes. She shaded them with her hand, trying to imagine what Miguel was talking about.

For a moment, she saw *un fantasma*, a ghost of Abuelita walking toward her, with one arm reaching out to her and the other pressing on a wooden cane.

"Esperanza," said the ghost.

She heard Hortensia suck in her breath.

Suddenly, Esperanza knew that her eyes were not deceiving her. Her throat tightened and she felt as if she couldn't move.

Abuelita came closer. She was small and wrinkled, with wisps of white hair falling out of her bun at the back of her head. Her clothes looked mussed from travel, but she had her same white lace handkerchief tucked into the sleeve of her dress and her eyes brimmed with tears. Esperanza tried to say her name but couldn't. Her throat was cramping from her emotions. She could only reach out for her grandmother and bury her head in the familiar smell of face powder, garlic, and peppermint.

"Abuelita, Abuelita!" she cried.

"*Aquí estoy*. I am here, *mi nieta*. How I have missed you."

Esperanza rocked her back and forth, daring to believe that it was true, looking at her through tears to make sure she was not dreaming. And laughing finally. Laughing and smiling and holding her hands. Then Hortensia and Alfonso took their turns.

Esperanza looked at Miguel.

"How?" she asked.

"I needed to have something to do while I waited for work. So I went for her."

After they pulled into camp, they escorted Abuelita into their cabin where they found Josefina, Juan, and the babies waiting.

"Josefina, where's Mama?"

"It was warm so we settled her in the shade. She fell asleep. Isabel is sitting with her. Is everything all right?"

Hortensia introduced Abuelita to Juan and Josefina, whose faces lit up. Esperanza then watched her grandmother look around the tiny room that now held pieces of their new life. Isabel's pictures on the wall, a bowl of peaches on the table, the babies' toys underfoot, Papa's roses in a coffee can. Esperanza wondered what Abuelita thought of the sad conditions, but she just smiled and said, "Please take me to my daughter."

Esperanza took Abuelita's hand and led her toward the trees. She could see Mama reclining in the shade near the wooden table. A quilt was spread on the ground nearby where the babies usually played. Isabel was running back from the vineyard, her hands full of wildflowers and grapevines. She saw Esperanza and ran toward her and Abuelita.

Isabel stopped in front of them, her face flushed and smiling.

"Isabel, this is Abuelita."

Isabel's eyes widened and her mouth popped open in surprise. "Do you really walk barefoot in the grapes and carry smooth stones in your pockets?"

Abuelita laughed, reached deep into the pocket of her dress, pulled out a flat, slick stone and gave it to Isabel. She looked at it in amazement, then handed Abuelita the wildflowers.

"I think you and I will be good friends, Isabel, yes?"

Isabel nodded and stepped aside so Abuelita could go to her daughter.

There was no way to prepare Mama.

Esperanza watched Abuelita walk to where Mama slept, resting on the makeshift lounge. She was framed by the vineyard, the grapes ripe and ready to drop.

Abuelita stopped a few feet from Mama and looked at her.

A stack of lace *carpetas* was at Mama's side as well as her crochet needle and thread. Abuelita reached out and stroked her hair, gently pulling the loose strands away from Mama's face and smoothing them against her head.

Softly, Abuelita said, "Ramona."

Mama did not open her eyes, but said as if she was dreaming, "Esperanza, is that you?"

"No, Ramona, it is me, Abuelita."

Mama slowly opened her eyes. She stared at Abuelita with no reaction, as if she was not really seeing her at all. Then she lifted her hand and reached out to touch her mother's face, making sure that the vision was true.

Abuelita nodded, "Yes, it is me. I have come."

Abuelita and Mama uttered no words that anyone could understand. It was their own language of happy exclamations and overwhelming emotions. Esperanza watched them cry and she wondered if her own heart would burst from so much joy.

"Oh, Esperanza!" said Isabel, jumping up and down and clapping. "I think my heart is dancing."

Esperanza barely choked out the whisper, "Mine, too." Then she picked up Isabel and spun her around in her arms.

Mama would not let go of Abuelita. She scooted over and made Abuelita sit next to her and held on to her arms as if she might disappear.

Suddenly, Esperanza remembered her promise, ran back to the cabin and returned, carrying something in her arms.

"Esperanza," said Abuelita, "Could that possibly be my blanket? Did you finish it?"

"Not yet," she said, unfolding the blanket.

Mama held one end, and Esperanza pulled the other end. It reached from the chinaberry tree to the mulberry. It could have covered three beds. They all laughed. The yarn was still connected, waiting for the last row to be finished.

They all gathered on the quilt and at the table. Esperanza sat down and pulled the massive blanket next to her, took the needle, and began crocheting the final stitches.

When Mama could finally speak, she looked at Abuelita and asked the same thing Esperanza had asked, "How did you get here?"

"Miguel," said Abuelita. "He came for me. Luis and Marco have been impossible. If I went to the market, one of their spies would follow me. I think they thought you were still in the area and would eventually come back for me."

Ten stitches up to the top of the mountain.

Esperanza listened to Abuelita tell Mama about how infuriated Tío Luis had been when he found out they were gone. He'd become obsessed with finding them and questioned all of their neighbors, including Señor Rodríguez. They had even come to the convent to question her sisters. But no one told him anything.

Add one stitch.

A few months after they left, she'd had a premonition that something was wrong with Mama. The feeling would not let go of her so she lit candles every day for months and prayed for their safety.

Nine stitches down to the bottom of the valley.

Then one day, when she had almost given up hope, she found an injured bird in the garden that she did not think would fly again, but the next morning when she approached it, the bird lifted into the sky. She knew it was a sign that whatever had been wrong, was better.

Skip one stitch.

Then one of the nuns brought her a note that someone had left in the poor box addressed to her. It had been from Miguel. He suspected that Abuelita was being watched so he delivered his notes after dark, telling her of his plan.

Ten stitches up to the top of the mountain.

Miguel and Señor Rodríguez came in the

middle of the night and took her to the train station. It was all very exciting. And Miguel didn't leave her side once during the entire trip. He brought her all the way here.

Add one stitch.

He said that Ramona and Esperanza needed her.

"He was right," said Mama, her eyes teary again, gratefully looking at Miguel.

Mountains and valleys. Mountains and valleys. So many of them, thought Esperanza. When a strand of her hair fell into her lap, she picked it up and wove it into the blanket, so that all of the happiness and emotion she felt at this moment would go with it forever.

When Esperanza told Abuelita their story, about all that had happened to them, she didn't measure time by the usual seasons. Instead, she told it as a field-worker, in spans of fruits and vegetables and by what needed to be done to the land.

They had arrived in the valley at the end of the grapes: Thompson seedless, Red Malagas, and the blue-black Ribiers. Mama breathed in the dust at the end of the grapes and that's when she got sick. Then it had been time to prune the grapes and get ready for potatoes. Working potatoes was the heart of winter and the cold that dampened the bones. And during potato eyes, Mama had gone to the hospital. There had been no months with names, only the time of tying canes amidst the ghosts of grapes and gray days that never warmed. But afterward came the anticipation of spring and a valley pregnant with needs: graceful asparagus, ripening vineyards, and groaning trees. Then early peaches called, crickets in the fields started their nightly symphonies, and Mama came home. Abuelita arrived during plums. And now, the grapes were delivering another harvest and Esperanza was turning another year.

A few days before her birthday, Esperanza begged Miguel to drive her to the foothills before sunrise. There was something she wanted to do. She woke in the dark and tiptoed from the cabin.

They followed the dirt road that headed east and parked when they could go no farther.

In the gray light, they could see a small footpath to a plateau.

When they got to the top, Esperanza looked out over the valley. The cool, almost-morning air filled her senses. Below, she could see the white roofs of the cabins in straight rows, the fields beginning to take form, and over the eastern mountains, a hopeful brightening.

She bent over and touched the grass. It was cool but dry. She lay down on her stomach and patted the ground next to her. "Miguel, did you know that if you lie on the ground and stay very still, you can feel the earth's heart beating?"

He looked at her skeptically.

She patted the ground again.

Then he lay down as she was, facing her.

"Will this happen soon, Esperanza?"

"*Aguántate tantito y la fruta caerá en tu mano.* Wait a little while and the fruit will fall into your hand."

He smiled and nodded.

They were still.

She watched Miguel watching her.

And then she felt it. Beginning softly. A gentle thumping, repeating itself. Then stronger. She heard it, too. *Shoomp. Shoomp. Shoomp.* The earth's heartbeat. Just like she had felt it that day with Papa.

Miguel smiled and she knew that he felt it, too.

The sun peeked over the rim of a distant ridge, bursting the dawn onto the waiting fields. She felt its warmth washing over her and turned on her back and faced the sky, staring into the clouds now tinged with pink and orange.

As the sun rose, Esperanza began to feel as if she rose with it. Floating again, like that day on the mountain, when she first arrived in the valley. She closed her eyes, and this time she did not careen out of control. Instead, she glided above the earth, unafraid. She let herself be lifted into the sky, and she knew that she would not slip away. She knew that she would never lose Papa or El Rancho de las Rosas, or Abuelita or Mama, no matter what happened. It was as Carmen, the egg woman, had said on the train. She had her family, a garden full of roses, her faith, and the memories of those who had gone before her. But now, she had even more than that, and it carried her up, as on the wings of the phoenix. She soared with the anticipation of dreams she never knew she could have, of learning English, of supporting her family, of someday buying a tiny house. Miguel had been right about never giving up, and she had been right, too, about rising above those who held them down.

She hovered high above the valley, its basin surrounded by the mountains. She swooped over Papa's rose blooms, buoyed by rosehips that remembered all the beauty they had seen. She waved at Isabel and Abuelita, walking barefoot in the vineyards, wearing grapevine wreaths in their hair. She saw Mama, sitting on a blanket, a cacaphony of color that covered an acre in zigzag rows. She saw Marta and her mother walking in an almond grove, holding hands. Then she flew over a river, a thrusting torrent that cut through the mountains. And there, in the middle of the wilderness, was a girl in a blue silk dress and a boy with his hair slicked down, eating mangoes on a stick, carved to look like exotic flowers, sitting on a grassy bank, on the same side of the river.

Esperanza reached for Miguel's hand and found it, and even though her mind was soaring to infinite possibilities, his touch held her heart to the earth.

~

"*Estas son las mañanitas que cantaba el Rey David*

*a las muchachas bonitas; se las cantamos aquí.*

*Despierta, mi bien, despierta. Mira que ya amaneció.*

*Ya los pajaritos cantan, la luna ya se metió.*

These are the morning songs which King David used to sing

to all the pretty girls; we sing them here to you.

Awake, my beloved, awake. See, it is already dawn.

The birds are already singing, the moon has already gone."

On the morning of her birthday, Esperanza heard the voices coming from outside her window. She could pick out Miguel's, Alfonso's, and Juan's.

She sat up in bed and listened. And smiled. Esperanza lifted the curtain. Isabel came over to her bed and looked out with her, clutching her doll. They both blew kisses to the men who sang the birthday song. Then Esperanza waved them inside, not to open gifts, but because she could already smell coffee coming from the kitchen.

They gathered for breakfast: Mama and Abuelita, Hortensia and Alfonso, Josefina and Juan, the babies and Isabel. Irene and Melina came, too, with their family. And Miguel. It wasn't exactly like the birthdays of her past. But it would still be a celebration, under the mulberry and chinaberry trees, with newborn rosebuds from Papa's garden. Although there were no papayas, there was cantaloupe, lime, and coconut salad. And *machaca burritos* topped with lots of laughter and teasing. At the end of the meal, Josefina brought out a *flan de almendras*, Esperanza's favorite, and they sang the birthday song to her again.

Isabel sat next to Abuelita at the wooden table. They each held crochet hooks and a skein of yarn. "Now watch, Isabel. Ten stitches up to the top of the mountain."

Abuelita demonstrated and Isabel carefully copied her movements.

The needle rocked awkwardly and at the end of her beginning rows, Isabel held up her work to show Esperanza. "Mine is all crooked!"

Esperanza smiled and reached over and gently pulled the yarn, unraveling the uneven stitches. Then she looked into Isabel's trusting eyes and said, "Do not ever be afraid to start over."

# Author's Note

I can still see my grandmother crocheting blankets in zigzag rows. She made one for each of her seven children, many of her twenty-three grandchildren (I am the eldest of the grandchildren), and for the great-grandchildren she lived to see. My grandmother, Esperanza Ortega, was the inspiration for this book.

When I was a young girl, Grandma used to tell me what her life was like when she first came to the United States from Mexico. I had heard stories about the company farm camp where she lived and worked, and the lifelong friends she made there. When she talked about those people and how they had helped her through desperate, trying times, she sometimes cried at the memories.

It wasn't until I had children of my own that my grandmother told me about her life in Mexico, about a fairy-tale existence with servants, wealth, and grandeur, which had preceded her life in the company farm camp. I wrote down some of her recollections from her childhood. How I wish I had written down more before she died because I could never stop wondering about her transition from Mexico to California and what it must have been like. Eventually, I started to imagine a story based on the girl who might have been her.

This fictional story parallels her life in some ways. She was born and raised in Aguascalientes, Mexico. Her father was Sixto Ortega and her mother, Ramona. They lived on El Rancho de la Trinidad (which I changed to El Rancho de las Rosas) and her uncles did hold prominent positions in the community. A series of circumstances, including her father's death, eventually forced my grandmother to immigrate to the United States to a company-owned farm labor camp in Arvin, California. Unlike Esperanza in the story, my grandmother had already married my grandfather, Jesús Muñoz, when she immigrated to California. Like Miguel, he had been her father's mechanic. In the segregated Mexican camp, with my grandfather, she lived much like the characters in the story. She washed her clothes in communal tubs, went to *jamaicas* on Saturday nights, and cared for her first three daughters. That's where my mother, Esperanza Muñoz, was born.

During the early 1930s there were many strikes in the California agricultural fields. Often, growers evicted the strikers from their labor camps, forcing many to live together in makeshift refugee camps, sometimes on farms on the outskirts of towns. The growers were powerful and could sometimes influence local governments. In Kern County, sheriffs arrested picketers for obstructing traffic, even though the roads were deserted. In Kings County, one Mexican man was arrested for speaking to a crowd in Spanish. Sometimes the strikes failed, especially in areas that were flooded with people from states like Oklahoma, who were desperate for work at any wage. In other instances, the strong voices of many people changed some of the pitiful conditions.

The Mexican Repatriation was very real and an often overlooked part of our history. In March of 1929, the federal government passed the

Deportation Act that gave counties the power to send great numbers of Mexicans back to Mexico. Government officials thought this would solve the unemployment associated with the Great Depression (it didn't). County officials in Los Angeles, California, organized "deportation trains" and the Immigration Bureau made "sweeps" in the San Fernando Valley and Los Angeles, arresting anyone who looked Mexican, regardless of whether or not they were citizens or in the United States legally. Many of those sent to Mexico were native-born United States citizens and had never been to Mexico. The numbers of Mexicans deported during this so-called "voluntary repatriation" was greater than the Native American removals of the nineteenth century and greater than the Japanese-American relocations during World War II. It was the largest involuntary migration in the United States up to that time. Between 1929 and 1935 at least 450,000 Mexicans and Mexican Americans were sent back to Mexico. Some historians think the numbers were closer to a million.

Even though my grandmother lived in this country for over fifty years, I can still remember her breaking out in nervous perspiration and trembling as her passport was checked at the border when we returned to the United States from a shopping trip in Tijuana. She always carried the fear that she could be sent back on a whim, even though repatriation had long been over.

My father, Don Bell, came to California during the Dust Bowl from the Midwest and, ironically, worked for the same company farm where my mother was born. By that time, my grandmother had moved her family to a small house in Bakersfield at 1030 P Street. Mom and Dad weren't destined to meet quite yet. Dad was twelve years old when he picked potatoes during World War II with the "Diaper Crew," children paid to pick the fields because of the great shortage of workers due to the war. He says the children weren't always the most diligent employees and admits he more often threw dirt clods at his friends than he picked potatoes. Later, when he was sixteen, he spent a summer working for the same farm, driving trucks back and forth from the fields and delivering workers.

Much of our nation's produce comes from this one area in California. It is hot in the summer and cold in the winter. There are dust storms and tule fog and some people do contract Valley Fever. Before I got married, I took the required blood test in San Diego where I had lived during my college years. The doctor called because of an "urgent finding" on my lab results. I worried that something dramatic had been found, until the doctor said, "You tested positive for Valley Fever."

I let out a sigh of relief. I grew up seeing lugs of grapes on kitchen tables. I picked plums, peaches, apricots, nectarines, persimmons, almonds, walnuts, and pecans from backyard trees. Every year in August, I saw the grapes laid down on the ground to make raisins the same way they've been made for generations. Lemons, tomatoes, or squash appeared on our doorstep from neighbors' or my grandmothers' gardens. I'd never been conscious of having any symptoms of Valley Fever. The only fever I recollected was my burning affection for my beginnings and belongings.

"Of course I tested positive," I said to the doctor. "I grew up in the San Joaquin Valley." I knew that I had been naturally immunized to the actual disease by merely living there, from the air I had breathed growing up.

My family's feelings for the company camp are deep-rooted and still filled with loyalty for their start in this country and for the jobs they had at a time when so many had none. Most of the people I interviewed who lived in the same camp with my grandmother held no grudges against the Oklahomans or others who competed for their jobs at that time. One man I interviewed said, "We were all so poor. The Okies, the Filipinos, they were poor, too. We all knew the feeling of wanting to work and feed our families. That was why it was so hard for so many of us to strike."

When I asked about prejudice I was told, "Sure there was prejudice, horrible prejudice, but that's how things were then."

Many struggled just to put food on the table and sometimes seemed to be resigned to the social issues of the time. They focused only on survival and put their hopes and dreams into their children's and grandchildren's futures.

That's what Grandma did. She survived. All of her children learned English and so did she. Some of her children went to college. One became a professional athlete, another a member of the United States Foreign Service; others became secretaries, a writer, an accountant. And her grandchildren: newscasters, social workers, florists, teachers, film editors, lawyers, small business owners, and another writer: me.

Our accomplishments were her accomplishments. She wished the best for all of us and rarely looked back on the difficulties of her own life.

It is no wonder that in Spanish, *esperanza* means "hope."

# CONNECTIONS

# *from* Little House on the Prairie

## Laura Ingalls Wilder

*Like Esperanza, Laura and her sister Mary set off on an exciting and dangerous journey to a new home far away. Laura's family is moving from the Wisconsin woods to the wide open prairies of nineteenth-century Kansas.*

Pet and Patty began to trot briskly, as if they were glad, too. Laura held tight to the wagon bow and stood up in the jolting wagon. Beyond Pa's shoulder and far across the waves of green grass she could see the trees, and they were not like any trees she had seen before. They were no taller than bushes.

"Whoa!" said Pa, suddenly. "Now which way?" he muttered to himself.

The road divided here, and you could not tell which was the more-traveled way. Both of them were faint wheel tracks in the grass. One went toward the west, the other sloped downward a little, toward the south. Both soon vanished in the tall, blowing grass.

"Better go downhill, I guess," Pa decided. "The creek's down in the bottoms. Must be this is the way to the ford." He turned Pet and Patty toward the south.

The road went down and up and down and up again, over gently curving land. The trees were nearer now, but they were no taller. Then Laura gasped and clutched the wagon bow, for almost under Pet's and Patty's noses there was no more blowing grass, there was no land at all. She looked beyond the edge of the land and across the tops of trees.

The road turned there. For a little way it went along the cliff's top, then it went sharply downward. Pa put on the brakes; Pet and Patty braced themselves backward and almost sat down. The wagon wheels slid onward, little by little lowering the wagon farther down the steep slope into the ground. Jagged cliffs of bare red earth rose up on both sides of the wagon. Grass waved along their tops but nothing grew on their seamed straight-up-and-down sides. They were hot, and heat came from them against Laura's face. The wind was still blowing overhead, but it did not blow down into this deep crack in the ground. The stillness seemed strange and empty.

Then once more the wagon was level. The narrow crack down which it had come opened into the bottom lands. Here grew the tall trees whose tops Laura had seen from the prairie above. Shady groves were scattered on the rolling meadows, and in the groves deer were lying down hardly to be seen among the shadows. The deer turned their heads toward the wagon, and curious fawns stood up to see it more clearly.

Laura was surprised because she did not see the creek. But the bottom lands were wide. Down here, below the prairie, there were gentle hills and open sunny places. The air was still and hot. Under the wagon wheels the ground was soft. In the sunny open spaces the grass grew thin, and deer had cropped it short.

For a while the high, bare cliffs of red earth stood up behind the wagon. But they were almost hidden behind hills and trees when Pet and Patty stopped to drink from the creek.

The rushing sound of the water filled the still air. All along the creek banks the trees hung over it and made it dark with shadows. In the middle it ran swiftly, sparkling silver and blue.

"This creek's pretty high," Pa said. "But I guess we can make it all right. You can see this is a ford, by the old wheel ruts. What do you say, Caroline?"

"Whatever you say, Charles," Ma answered. Pet and Patty lifted their wet noses. They pricked their ears forward, looking at the creek; then they pricked them backward to hear what Pa would say. They sighed and laid their soft noses together to whisper to each other. A little way upstream, Jack was lapping the water with his red tongue.

"I'll tie down the wagon-cover," Pa said. He climbed down from the seat, unrolled the canvas sides and tied them firmly to the wagon box. Then he pulled the rope at the back, so that the canvas puckered together in the middle, leaving only a tiny round hole, too small to see through.

Mary huddled down on the bed. She did not like fords; she was afraid of the rushing water. But Laura was excited; she liked the splashing. Pa climbed to the seat, saying, "They may have to swim, out there in the middle. But we'll make it all right, Caroline."

Laura thought of Jack and said, "I wish Jack could ride in the wagon, Pa."

Pa did not answer. He gathered the reins tightly in his hands. Ma said, "Jack can swim, Laura. He will be all right."

The wagon went forward softly in mud. Water began to splash against the wheels. The splashing grew louder. The wagon shook as the noisy water struck at it. Then all at once the wagon lifted and balanced and swayed. It was a lovely feeling.

The noise stopped, and Ma said, sharply, "Lie down, girls!"

Quick as a flash, Mary and Laura dropped flat on the bed. When Ma spoke like that, they did as they were told. Ma's arm pulled a smothering blanket over them, heads and all.

"Be still, just as you are. Don't move!" she said.

Mary did not move; she was trembling and still. But Laura could not help wriggling a little bit. She did so want to see what was happening. She could feel the wagon swaying and turning; the splashing was noisy again, and again it died away. Then Pa's voice frightened Laura. It said, "Take them, Caroline!"

The wagon lurched; there was a sudden heavy splash beside it. Laura sat straight up and clawed the blanket from her head.

Pa was gone. Ma sat alone, holding tight to the reins with both hands. Mary hid her face in the blanket again, but Laura rose up farther. She couldn't see the creek bank. She couldn't see any thing in front of the wagon but water rushing at it. And in the water, three heads; Pet's head and Patty's head and Pa's small, wet head. Pa's fist in the water was holding tight to Pet's bridle.

Laura could faintly hear Pa's voice through the rushing of the water. It sounded calm and cheerful, but she couldn't hear what he said. He was talking to the horses. Ma's face was white and scared.

"Lie down, Laura," Ma said.

Laura lay down. She felt cold and sick. Her eyes were shut tight, but she could still see the terrible water and Pa's brown beard drowning in it.

For a long, long time the wagon swayed and swung, and Mary cried without making a sound and Laura's stomach felt sicker and sicker. Then the front wheels struck and grated, and Pa shouted. The whole wagon jerked and jolted and tipped backward, but the wheels were turning on the ground. Laura was up again, holding to the seat; she saw Pet's and Patty's scrambling wet backs climbing a steep bank, and Pa running beside them, shouting, "Hi, Patty! Hi, Pet! Get up! Get up! Whoopsy-daisy! Good girls!

At the top of the bank they stood still, panting and dripping. And the wagon stood still, safely out of the creek.

Pa stood panting and dripping, too, and Ma said, "Oh, Charles!"

"There, there, Caroline," said Pa. "We're all safe, thanks to a good tight wagon-box well fastened to the running-gear. I never saw a creek rise so fast in my life. Pet and Patty are good swimmers, but I guess they wouldn't have made it if I hadn't helped them."

If Pa had not known what to do, or if Ma had been too frightened to drive, or if Laura and Mary had been naughty and bothered her, then they would all have been lost. The river would have rolled them over and over and carried them away and drowned them, and nobody would ever have known what became of them. For weeks, perhaps, no other person would come along that road.

"Well," said Pa, "all's well that ends well," and Ma said, "Charles, you're wet to the skin."

Before Pa could answer, Laura cried, "Oh, where's Jack?"

They had forgotten Jack. They had left him on the other side of that dreadful water and they could not see him anywhere. He must have tried to swim after them, but they could not see him struggling in the water now.

Laura swallowed hard, to keep from crying.

She knew it was shameful to cry, but there was crying inside her. All the long way from Wisconsin poor Jack had followed them so patiently and faithfully, and now they had left him to drown. He was so tired, and they might have taken him into the wagon. He had stood on the bank and seen the wagon going away from him, as if they didn't care for him at all. And he would never know how much they wanted him.

Pa said he wouldn't have done such a thing to Jack, not for a million dollars. If he'd known how that creek would rise when they were in midstream, he would never have let Jack try to swim it. "But that can't be helped now," he said.

He went far up and down the creek bank, looking for Jack, calling him and whistling for him.

It was no use. Jack was gone.

At last there was nothing to do but to go on. Pet and Patty were rested. Pa's clothes had dried on him while he searched for Jack. He took the reins again, and drove uphill, out of the river bottoms.

Laura looked back all the way. She knew she wouldn't see Jack again, but she wanted to. She didn't see anything but low curves of land coming between the wagon and the creek, and beyond the creek those strange cliffs of red earth rose up again.

Then other bluffs just like them stood up in front of the wagon. Faint wheel tracks went into a crack between those earthen walls. Pet and Patty climbed till the crack became a small grassy valley. And the valley widened out to the High Prairie once more.

No road, not even the faintest trace of wheels or of a rider's passing, could be seen anywhere. That prairie looked as if no human eye had ever seen it before. Only the tall wild grass covered the endless empty land and a great empty sky arched over it. Far away the sun's edge touched the rim of the earth. The sun was enormous and it was throbbing and pulsing with light. All around the sky's edge ran a pale pink glow, and above the blue the sky was no color at all. Purple shadows were gathering over the land, and the wind was mourning.

Pa stopped the mustangs. He and Ma got out of the wagon to make camp, and Mary and Laura climbed down to the ground, too.

"Oh, Ma," Laura begged, "Jack has gone to heaven, hasn't he? He was such a good dog, can't he go to heaven?"

Ma did not know what to answer, but Pa said: "Yes, Laura, he can. God that doesn't forget the sparrows won't leave a good dog like Jack out in the cold."

Laura felt only a little better. She was not happy. Pa did not whistle about his work as usual, and after a while he said, "And what we'll do in a wild country without a good watch dog I don't know."

■ ■ ■

# Cesar Chavez
## Gloria D. Miklowitz

*If the United Farm Workers of America labor union had*
*existed when Esperanza and her family arrived in California,*
*their lives might have been a great deal easier. Cesar Chavez*
*was the former migrant worker who founded the UFW. He is*
*now regarded as one of the great labor leaders of American*
*history.*

The fruits and vegetables we eat do not arrive by magic in
our supermarkets. The tomatoes, corn, apples, lettuce and
grapes are planted on large farms by workers. When the
crop is ripe, it is picked by men, women and children who
move from farm to farm as needed. These "pickers" are
called "migrant" workers. Many come from Mexico and
speak only Spanish. Cesar Chavez was a migrant worker
who knew firsthand how hard life was for his people.
As an adult, he brought people together into the United
Farm Workers Union to fight for better working and
living conditions.

After he was born in 1927 in Yuma, Ariz., Chavez's early
years were easy. His father farmed land inherited from his
father. The family grew corn and beans, melons and other
fruits and vegetables. They sold what they didn't eat to pay
for other needs. As Chavez and his five sisters and brothers
grew, they helped in the fields. When Chavez was 10 years
old, the United States was in deep trouble because of the
Great Depression. There were few jobs. People could not
find work to feed their families. There was little rain so the
crops did poorly. With little money coming in, Chavez's
father could not pay the taxes on his land. The state took
over his farm. How would the family live?

Many other farmers faced the same problem: They would do anything to earn enough to feed their families. Men, called "labor contractors," came from California. They told poor farmers that in California they could earn good money going from one farm to another picking produce. Chavez's parents and many others decided to leave Arizona. They rolled up their mattresses, roped their belongings together and loaded everything on the roofs of their old cars. They hoped that in California they would earn enough so their children would not have to work and could go to school.

\* \* \*

California looked wonderful to the Chavez family. There were lush fields of growing things. Life would be good here, they thought. Cesar Chavez's father drove to the large farm where he was told they could find jobs. Old, one-room shacks made of sheet metal would be their home. There was no running water, no bathroom, only one gas burner to cook on, and unbearable heat. They unpacked, brought water in buckets from a faucet in the yard, ate a cold meal and slept on the floor that first night.

The next day the Chavez family went to work in the fields. Often the only drinking water was what they brought along. Pickers had to bend over all day. Many crops had been dusted with poisons to kill insects. The poison made some workers sick. They worked long hours and were not always paid what they had been promised. Since most workers could not speak English, they could not argue.

For years this was the life Chavez and his family lived. They moved from farm to farm, wherever the labor contractors sent them. When not in school, Chavez worked in the fields with his parents. By the time he finished the eighth grade, he had attended more than 30 schools. Since migrant students did not stay long in one place and couldn't speak much English, they had a hard time in school.

As Chavez learned English, he could speak with non-Latino workers. From them he found out which farms paid best, where housing was better, and where the owners did not cheat the workers. He told other Mexican American families what he learned so they would not suffer as he and his family had. He tried to persuade them to go together to the farm owners and ask for more pay and better housing. Most workers turned him down, afraid they would lose their jobs. But he wouldn't give up. Thus began Cesar Chavez's crusade to improve the lives of farm workers.

*     *     *

As Cesar Chavez grew older, he found work in the vineyards, which required year-round tending. When he was 15, he met Helen Fabela, who also worked in the fields. They fell in love and shared the same goals, but it was wartime, and they were too young to marry. In 1944, at 17, Cesar enlisted in the Navy and served in the western Pacific. When he returned to California, after the war, he found that migrant workers' lives had not changed. Helen and Cesar married in 1948 and moved to San Jose. Cesar worked in apricot orchards and a lumberyard. They lived in a barrio, called "Sal Si Puedes" in Spanish. In English, this means "get out if you can."

Two men became important to Cesar: Father Donald McDonnell, who, with his church, helped people with daily problems; and Fred Ross, who started the Community Service Organization to help residents solve their own problems. Cesar first volunteered, then worked for, the CSO. He organized teams to register voters. He battled racial and economic discrimination and built new CSO chapters across California and Arizona. During this time, he read a lot about politics and about leaders who believed in nonviolence as a way to accomplish change. Cesar believed strongly that farm workers needed an organization that would help them. He tried to persuade the CSO to fill that need, but failed. Using $1,200 of his and Helen's savings, and loans and gifts from friends and relatives, he resigned from his paid job and formed the National Farm Workers Association. In 11 months, he visited 87 communities and held many gatherings to get workers to join the union. When 300 members were signed up, he called a meeting. If each family paid a small amount, he said, the union could open grocery stores, drugstores and gas stations where workers could buy things cheap. It could hire lawyers to represent them; it could even lend money. He wanted all activities to be nonviolent, and he took no pay while working long hours. Food and clothing for his family of eight children came from donations. Even his children helped by handing out leaflets.

* * *

Farm workers had no laws to protect them. Unscrupulous growers could pay them as little as they liked; they could make them work long hours without rest breaks, with no water to drink, or toilets, among poison-sprayed plants. They did not have to give them clean places to live. With membership growing and money coming in, Chavez did as he had promised, but then planned more. As soon as the National Farm Workers grew big enough, he urged members to demand the pay and conditions that other workers in America enjoyed. In 1965, grape pickers who were not association members got angry. They needed more money during harvest season because in winter there would be no work. They demanded $1.40 an hour and 25 cents for each box of grapes picked.

"We will stop working," they threatened. "Your grapes will rot on the vines!" The pickers lined up at the edge of the fields and shouted *"Huelga!"* which means "strike" in Spanish. At first Chavez did not want his union to join the strike. His members would need food and the union had very little money to help. Still, his followers urged him to join and soon union members lined the fields shouting *"Huelga!"* too. For weeks, owners and strikers argued. Finally two vineyards agreed to raise wages and the strikers there went back to work. But other growers brought in workers from Mexico to pick the grape crop. These workers accepted the bad pay and poor conditions. The strike went on for many months. Money and help came from people who read about the strike and believed in what Chavez was doing. But the grape growers would not give in. Then, one day, Chavez had an idea. He would hit them where it really hurt—in the pocketbook.

A strike against growers didn't work. The vineyard owners brought in temporary pickers from Mexico. Those laborers went home when the harvest ended, feeling rich with the few dollars they made. "What if," Cesar Chavez reasoned, "the whole country got behind the strikers and refused to buy table grapes or wine?" That would be a boycott—similar to what Mahatma Gandhi did with salt in India[1].

"Don't Buy California Grapes!" became a slogan carried on signs, posted in stores and written about in newspapers. Truck drivers refused to take grapes from vineyards to stores or to load them on ships to send to other countries. Chavez fasted (went without food) for 25 days, only drinking water. It was the first of other fasts to bring attention to the migrant workers' cause. The grape boycott involved groups and

---

1. Mohandas Gandhi (1869–1948), known as "Mahatma," or "Great Soul"; Indian nationalist leader. In 1930 he led a nationwide protest against a tax on salt.

people from all over the country. It hurt growers, as Chavez predicted, in their "pocketbooks." Without violence, it forced them to agree to some of the workers' demands.

*   *   *

In 1972, Chavez's union became the United Farm Workers of America, part of the AFL-CIO, a powerful group of many labor unions. As UFW president, Chavez earned very little and worked 14-hour days. Joining with the new union brought about benefits such as a medical plan, an education fund, pension money for retirement, better working conditions and a way for workers to voice complaints. But not all has been won. Though the short-handled hoe has been outlawed because of the back problems it can cause, it is still in use. The program of importing foreign workers from Mexico ended, but the problem continues. Union membership has dropped off though the UFW still negotiates farm worker contracts.

Chavez died in 1993 at age 66. More than 50,000 mourners came to honor him. At a White House ceremony on Aug. 8, 1994, President Clinton presented the Presidential Medal of Freedom to Helen Chavez, in honor of her husband. Clinton said that Chavez "faced formidable, often violent opposition with dignity and nonviolence."

This year, a bill was passed declaring March 31 a day to honor Chavez. State workers will enjoy a paid holiday. Public schools and courts are not included. Neither are farm workers. Nevertheless, many California schoolchildren will spend the day learning about Chavez's life and doing community service. It will be the first American holiday honoring a Latino leader.

©2000 Los Angeles Times

# A List of 10 Things
## Loubel Cruz

*Like Esperanza, Colleen Marshall makes a big move in her life. Although the difficulties she faces are somewhat less serious than those faced by Esperanza, they still require her to do a lot of growing up. Loubel Cruz was a student at Klein Forest High School in Houston, Texas, when she wrote this story.*

There is a window right next to my seat in sixth period literature that offers a view of the courtyard. Good thing, that window, for if it wasn't there, I would be asleep. I listened restlessly to Sister Mary Catherine lecture on and on about who the main characters were in *A Tale of Two Cities*. I watched the snow gently falling on the statue of St. Francis of Assisi, the patron saint after whom my school was named, amazed at how much snow had already accumulated. It was the beginning of February, and, being a native Texan, I was not used to foot-deep snow packs on my sidewalk every morning. But that's what you get when you move to Boston—home of the Red Sox, commercial fishing, and blizzards. I smiled at that thought, for it was exactly what Davis warned me about before I moved here, except he probably didn't know how right he was. I laughed inside when I thought of Davis. Then my heart began to hurt when I thought of Davis. Then my heart began to hurt when I thought about how the move here was the most difficult thing I'd ever done. It all started above five months ago. Five months ago when the biggest event in my short, but unpredictable, fifteen years began.

It was a hot, humid day in October. The kind of day you wish the air conditioner was going full blast and that there was more ice in your lemonade and that you'd put on more deodorant that morning. I was living in Houston, Texas, where I'd lived all my life, and attended Duke Senior High, where I was a freshman.

"My parents are acting weird, all secretive and stuff," I told Davis Vaughn. It was worrying me, it really was.

We were sitting in my room after school and Davis was checking, or should I say copying, my geometry answers. He didn't like math, and never really tried at it. His favorite subject was gym. Davis was convinced he was going to become all-pro in every sport that ever existed and become a "kabillionaire." And even though he taunted me about my dream, which was to become a writer, I never once thought of shattering his hopes.

"Look, Marshall, everything will be OK. Your parents have just been hanging around mine too much. It makes them wacko too," Davis said, not taking his eyes off the postulates and theorems.

A couple of years ago he came up with this wonderful idea to call me by my last name—which is Marshall—instead of my first—which is Colleen. He said Colleen was too feminine. I said I was a girl. He said he wasn't sure. I said for him to stuff it. It was all annoying at first, but I got used to it.

Davis Vaughn is my best friend. I never really told him that, and now that I think of it, I never admitted it to anyone else; I bet he never has either. But we knew. We knew deep down and our friendship was so strong we didn't have to say it.

"Well, I'd better be going home now," Davis said, closing the geometry book. "It's broccoli quiche night. Don't worry, Marshall, everything will be cool."

I looked at him, storm clouds in my eyes.

"I promise." He smiled at me, his eyes sparkling. The "Davis sparkle," as I called it.

That night at dinner, I played with my food, occasionally forcing a small piece of lasagna down my throat. My parents kept looking at me funny, very curious about what my problem was. Good, that's what I wanted; I wanted to know what was wrong, too.

"Colleen, sweetie, is anything wrong?" my mom asked, putting more food on my plate, pretending not to notice the unfinished pieces that were still there.

I shook my head.

My parents exchanged worried glances and then, after a while, my father spoke. "Collie, there's something we have been wanting to tell you."

I swallowed hard. Oh no, here it comes! I thought of every bad thing that could have happened.

"We're moving."

"Huh?" I knew what he said; I just wanted to pretend he didn't say it, hoping I was wrong. Funny, that wasn't one of the things I thought he might say.

My father looked at my mom nervously and then looked at me, forcing a weak smile. "Bennett and Foresman have opened up a new firm in Boston. And, well . . . they picked me to manage it. Collie, it's the chance of a lifetime, one that I've been waiting for."

I stared. Not at my parents, but down, at my hands. Davis once said, jokingly, that I had beautiful hands. But in a way, I thought he meant it. My hands were sweating now. They were nervous. Davis would have been disappointed.

"Collie?" my mom said, concerned. "It's going to be great, sweetie, I promise. There will be lots of snow. You always loved snow." She was talking to me as if I was a two-year-old. It must have been already determined.

After a couple of unbearable minutes of silence, I opened my mouth but nothing came out. Finally a voice whispered, "Boston? When?"

"We want to have you ready for the second semester, so we want to move during the Christmas vacation."

I don't remember who answered me, and I don't remember starting to cry, either. I do recall my mom handing me a pink Kleenex which I refused to accept, and the strained expression on my father's face, as if he'd just ruined my adolescence forever.

"Uh, Mom, I have some homework. Could I . . ."

"Sure, sweetie, go ahead."

I walked slowly to my room and closed the door behind me. Almost instinctively, I picked up the phone by my bed and waited for the person on the other end to make my tears stop.

"Hello?"

"Hello, Davis?"

"Marshall? Hey, what's up?"

I didn't answer. I was thinking.

"Marshall? Everything OK? Marrshhaal!"

"Yeah, everything's cool." I couldn't tell him. I was depressed . . . and scared. "Just wanted to know if you had a game tomorrow."

"Yup. Playing King Memorial. We're gonna get creamed." I already knew that.

"Okay, I was just wondering. Bye."

"Later."

I got up and began to pace. I didn't know how to feel, act, or what to say. It really started to tick me off. I felt a tear form in my eye and quickly brushed it away. When I start to cry, I never can stop. But those stupid tears kept forming, multiplying by the second. They fell down my face, leaving black streaks of mascara under my eyes. Then the crying turned into sobs, deep hard chokes that could not be controlled. I fell onto my bed, buried my head in the pillow, and, still crying, fell asleep.

The next afternoon found Davis and me in my room, engaged in our daily ritual of me doing geometry and Davis copying it. The day had been terrible. I spent most of it trying to avoid my friends and trying not to cry. Davis knew something was wrong, but was smart enough not to ask what it was. I knew I had to tell him, though.

"I'm moving."

"Hmmmm?" He was too caught up in trying to get the altitude length of a right triangle.

"I'm moving."

"Yeah, right."

"Davis," I said angrily, reaching over the bed and slamming the geometry book closed. "I'm serious."

Davis looked at me hard, straight into my eyes.

After what seemed an eternity, he looked down. He knew the truth.

"Where?"

"Boston."

"When?"

"Christmas vacation."

Finally his eyes met mine. The "Davis sparkle" wasn't in them.

"Why?"

I started to feel my heart knot. "It's not my decision."

Davis looked down and pretended to be engrossed in the design of my bedspread. He said nothing, but I knew exactly how he felt. Finally, without looking up he spoke.

"Boston's pretty cool, I guess. The Red Sox and all. There's gonna be a lot of snow. You can ice-skate a lot." He picked up the geometry book and continued to study.

"Geez, Davis, you sound like my mother." I was getting angry now. He acted like he didn't care.

"Well, geez, Colleen, what do you want me to say? That I'm really glad you're moving so I can hang out with Herman Waltflower? I can't say what I want. I can't say don't go because I know you have to." There was anger and confusion in his eyes. I had never seen him this way. It scared me—he called me Colleen.

"It's not my fault," I said, the tears starting to flow.

"Look, I gotta go now. It's getting late." Davis got up, gathered his things, and without another word, left, slamming the door behind him.

I didn't cry that night. I was too mad—at everybody. At my dad for accepting a job thousands of miles away, at my mom for agreeing to go along with it, at Davis for being such a lousy friend when I needed him most, and at me for being mad and not crying.

The next day I tried to find Davis to talk to him, but at the same time tried to avoid his presence. The first time I saw him was in Mrs. Drew's English class. He didn't look my way, so I tried not to look his. We were studying poetry, and our assignment for the day was to write a list of ten things. God only knows how that is poetry, but I was too preoccupied to think about it. I looked over at Davis to see if he would give me one of his this-is-such-a-stupid-class looks, but he didn't. He just stared straight ahead, very intent on what Mrs. Drew was saying. He didn't talk to me for the rest of the school day.

That afternoon the doorbell rang. I was too busy lying on my bed being depressed to answer it, but then I remembered no one was home. I lazily opened the door.

"Could you help me with geometry? I have no idea what's going on." Davis gave me a shy grin and invited himself inside.

"Davis, I'm sorry. I really shouldn't have . . ."

"Hey, Marshall, forget about it. It's not your fault. I should be the one who's sorry. Boston, huh? No offense, but you're gonna freeze your rear up there."

I laughed. This was the way it should have been.

"Let's not talk about you moving anymore, OK?

"Promise?"

"Promise."

Davis smiled, satisfied. "So what did you think about Drew's poem today? I wrote ten reasons why the Oilers never made it to the Super Bowl. What a stupid class."

And that was that.

Two months came and went. And as we promised, Davis and I didn't mention anything about moving. He helped me pack, but we never actually discussed why. We went on with our daily routine as if I wasn't leaving: him copying geometry, me watching his football games, him proofreading my newspaper articles.

Then the day before moving day came. We were in my room comparing Christmas presents. We laughed, talked, and gossiped, but we knew the time to say goodbye was coming nearer.

"Uh, well, Merry Christmas," he said, giving me a small wrapped box.

"Thanks," I said, opening the gift. I already gave him my present that morning, which I don't think he really liked—but he did a really good job of acting like he did.

Inside the box was a golden locket. It was beautiful.

"Uh, my mom picked it out because you know how I am with girl presents," he said laughing. "I thought you would like it, though. I didn't put my picture in it 'cause you might find a really cute guy up there in Massachusetts. But there's something engraved in it so you won't forget me."

"Thanks." I immediately put it on. I loved it.

"Oh, here's another thing." He gave me a small envelope. He smiled. "This is really from me. Don't open it yet, though. After I leave."

I wanted to ask why, but I just nodded obediently.

"Well, I gotta go now. It's getting late." He got up awkwardly and headed for the door. "Boston will be awesome, Marshall. I promise. You'll be fine." He smiled at me.

"Bye."

"Later." Davis opened my bedroom door.

I felt tears running down my face. "I love you, Davis."

He turned around and smiled. His eyes sparkled with little teardrops ready to fall. "I know, Marshall.' And with that he walked away.

I closed my door and let the dam break. I sat down on the floor, and through the tears read what Davis had written.

## TEN THINGS COLLEEN K. MARSHALL SHOULD ALWAYS REMEMBER IN BOSTON

1) Don't get one of those gross New England accents.
2) In association with #1, say "ya'll" as much as possible.
3) She's beautiful.

4) Even if she's in Boston, she will always be a Texan at heart.

5) Her name is Marshall.

6) No matter what anyone tells her, she's going to be a writer. She will write only the truth.

7) It's not her fault if a certain person flunks geometry. Ha, Ha.

8) She's not fat, she's not fat, she's not fat.

9) Oilers rule!

10) And the last thing Colleen K. Marshall should always remember in Boston is that even though he never says it, Davis R. Vaughn loves her too.

How could he write this? He knew I would cry. Despite all my tears, I found myself laughing. Laughing at what he wrote and all the good times we had. Davis knew me so well, better than anyone else, and I was leaving him. But as the gold locket said, "We'll always be together."

So here I am in Boston, going to a Catholic private school (thank heaven it's coed), wearing a red plaid uniform I wouldn't be caught dead wearing in Houston, and shoveling snow from my driveway every morning.

The bell rang. I slowly gathered my things from Sister Mary Catherine's literature class and walked out the door. I hadn't made many friends here—well, I really hadn't tried that hard—so it surprised me when I heard someone call my name down the hallway. I turned and saw a guy running toward me, panting.

"Hi, I'm Richard Luis. I'm the editor of the newspaper here. Call me Rick, though."

"Oh, hi. I'm Colleen Marshall. Call me . . ." I thought about it, "Colleen."

"I know." I felt surprised and kind of flattered that he did. "Sister Agnes says you're a very talented writer. We heard that you were on the news staff at your old school . . . in Texas?"

"Yes I was, in Houston."

"Houston, huh? The Oilers are pretty good."

I smiled, choking back a giggle.

"Well, anyway," he continued, "we really need some good writers, so I was wondering if you'd like to be on the staff."

"Yeah, that would be great." I couldn't believe my luck.

"Cool. What do you write?"

I thought of the list of ten things, which reminded me of Davis. "Only the truth."

From *Merlyn's Pen: Fiction, Essays, and Poems*
by America's Teens

■ ■ ■

# Ellis Island

## Marc Cohn

*More than 17 million immigrants came to America through Ellis Island in New York Harbor between 1892 and 1924. Singer Marc Cohn wrote this song to honor their memory.*

I was driving down Ninth Avenue
As the sky was getting dark
Didn't have nothin' else to do
So I kept on riding to Battery Park
I stepped out in the damp and misty night
As the fog was rolling in
Man said, "Last boat leaving tonight
Is the boat for Ellis Island"

As my feet touched solid ground
I felt a chill run down my spine
I could almost hear the sound
of thousands pushing through the lines
Mothers and bewildered wives
that sailed across the raging sea
Others running for their lives
to the land of opportunity
Down on Ellis Island

"What is this strange paradise?"
They must've wondered through their cries and moans
After all they've sacrificed
Their faith, their families, friends and homes
Then on the Inspection Stairs
They were counted out or counted in
Frozen while the inspectors stared
Down on Ellis Island

Now me I only stumbled in
Just to wander around that empty hall
Where someone else's fate had been
Decided in no time at all
And cases filled with hats and clothes
And the belongings of those who journeyed far
They're strange reminders I suppose
Of where we're from and who we are

But as the boat pulled off the shore
I could see the fog was lifting
And lights I never seen before
Were shining down on Ellis Island
Shining down on Ellis Island.

■ ■ ■

# The Winter Hibiscus
## Minfong Ho

*Like Esperanza Ortega, Saeng Panouvong has exchanged her own ancient culture for a new life in America. Now she has to face the American teenager's ultimate challenge: the driving test.*

Saeng stood in the open doorway and shivered as a gust of wind swept past, sending a swirl of red maple leaves rustling against her legs. Early October, and already the trees were being stripped bare. A leaf brushed against Saeng's sleeve, and she snatched at it, briefly admiring the web of dark veins against the fiery red, before letting it go again, to be carried off by the wind.

Last year she had so many maple leaves pressed between her thick algebra textbook that her teacher had suggested gently that she transfer the leaves to some other books at home. Instead, Saeng had simply taken the carefully pressed leaves out and left them in a pile in her room, where they moldered, turned smelly and were eventually tossed out. Saeng felt a vague regret, but no anger.

For a moment Saeng stood on the doorstep and watched the swirl of autumn leaves in the afternoon sunlight, thinking of the bleak winter ahead. She had lived through enough of them now to dread their grayness and silence and endless bone-chilling cold. She buttoned up her coat and walked down the worn path through their yard and toward the sidewalk.

*"Bai sai?"* her mother called to her, straightening up from neat rows of hot peppers and snow peas that were growing in the vacant lot next door.

"To take my driving test," Saeng replied in English.

Saeng remembered enough Laotian to understand just about everything her parents said to her, but she felt more comfortable now speaking in English. In the four years since they had migrated to America, they had evolved a kind of bilingual dialogue, where her parents would continue to address her brothers and her in Laotian, and they would reply in English, with each side sometimes slipping into the other's language to convey certain key words that seemed impossible to translate.

*"Luuke ji fao bai hed yang?"* her mother asked.

"There's no rush," Saeng conceded. "I just want to get there in plenty of time."

"You'll get there much too soon, and then what? You'll just stand around fretting and making yourself tense," Mrs. Panouvong continued in Laotian. "Better that you should help me harvest some of these melons."

Saeng hesitated. How could she explain to her mother that she wanted to just "hang out" with the other schoolmates who were scheduled to take the test that afternoon, and to savor the tingle of anticipation when David Lambert would drive up in his old blue Chevy and hand her the car keys?

"The last of the hot peppers should be picked, and the kale covered with a layer of mulch," Mrs. Panouvong added, wiping one hand across her shirt and leaving a streak of mud there.

Saeng glanced down at her own clean clothes. She had dressed carefully for the test—and for David. She had on a gray wool skirt and a Fair Isles sweater, both courtesy of David's mother from their last rummage sale at the church. And she had combed out her long black hair and left it hanging straight down her back the way she had seen the blond cheerleaders do theirs, instead of bunching it up with a rubber band.

"Come help your mother a little. *Mahteh, luuke*—Come on, child," her mother said gently.

There were certain words that held a strange resonance for Saeng, as if there were whispered echoes behind them. *Luuke,* or child, was one of these words. When her mother called her luuke in that soft, teasing way, Saeng could hear the voices of her grandmother, and her uncle, or her primary-school teachers behind it, as if there were an invisible chorus of smiling adults calling her, chiding her.

"Just for a while," Saeng said, and walked over to the melons, careful not to get her skirt tangled in any vines.

Together they worked in companionable silence for some time. The frost had already killed the snow peas and Chinese cabbage, and Saeng helped pluck out the limp brown stems and leaves. But the bitter melons, knobby and green, were still intact and ready to be harvested. Her mother had been insistent on planting only vegetables that weren't readily available at the local supermarkets, sending away for seeds from various Chinatowns as far away as New York and San Francisco. At first alone, then joined by the rest of her family, she had hoed the hard dirt of the vacant lot behind their dilapidated old house and planted the seeds in neat rows.

That first summer, their family had also gone smelting every night while the vast schools of fish were swimming upriver to spawn and had caught enough to fill their freezer full of smelt. And at dawn, when the dew was still thick on the grass, they had also combed the golf course at the country club for nightcrawlers, filling up large buckets with worms that they would sell later to the roadside grocery stores as fishbait. The money from selling the worms enabled them to buy a hundred-pound sack of the best long-grain fragrant rice, and that, together with the frozen smelt and homegrown vegetables, had lasted them through most of their first winter.

"America has opened her doors to us as guests," Saeng's mother had said. "We don't want to sit around waiting for its handouts like beggars." She and Mr. Panouvong had swallowed their pride and gotten jobs as a dishwasher and a janitor, and they were taking English lessons at night under a state program that, to their amazement, actually paid them for studying!

By the end of their second year, they were off welfare and were saving up for a cheap secondhand car, something that they could never have been able to afford as grade school teachers back in Laos.

And Saeng, their oldest child, had been designated their family driver.

"So you will be taking the driving test in the Lambert car?" Mrs. Panouvong asked now, adeptly twisting tiny hot peppers from their stems.

Saeng nodded. "Not their big station wagon, but the small blue car—David's." There it was again, that flutter of excitement as she said David's name. And yet he had hardly spoken to her more than two or three times, and each time only at the specific request of his mother.

Mrs. Lambert—their sponsor into the United States— was a large, genial woman with a ready smile and two brown braids wreathed around her head. The wife of the Lutheran minister in their town, she had already helped sponsor two Laotian refugee families and seemed to have enough energy and good will to sponsor several more. Four years ago, when they had first arrived, it was she who had taken the Panouvong family on their rounds of medical check-ups, social welfare interviews, school enrollments, and housing applications.

And it was Mrs. Lambert who had suggested, after
Saeng had finished her driver education course, that she
use David's car to take her driving test. Cheerfully, David—
a senior on the school basketball team—had driven Saeng
around and taken her for a few test runs in his car to famil-
iarize her with it. Exciting times they might have been for
Saeng—it was the closest she had ever come to being
on a date—but for David it was just something he was
doing out of deference to his mother. Saeng had no illu-
sions about this. Nor did she really mind it. It was enough
for her at this point just to vaguely pretend at dating. At
sixteen, she did not really feel ready for some of the
things most thirteen-year-olds in America seemed to be
doing. Even watching MTV sometimes made her wince
in embarrassment.

"He's a good boy, David is," Saeng's mother said, as if
echoing Saeng's thoughts. "Listens to his mother and father."
She poured the hot peppers from her cupped palm to a
woven basket and looked at Saeng. "How are you going to
thank him for letting you use his car and everything?"

Saeng considered this. "I'll say thank you, I guess. Isn't
that enough?"

"I think not. Why don't you buy for him a Big Mac?"
Big Mac was one of the few English words Mrs. Panouvong
would say, pronouncing it *Bee-Maag*. Ever since her husband had taken them to a McDonald's as a treat after his
first pay raise, she had thought of Big Macs as the epitome
of everything American.

To her daughter's surprise, she fished out a twenty-dollar
bill from her coat pocket now and held it out to Saeng. "You
can buy yourself one too. A Bee-Maag."

Saeng did not know what to say. Here was a woman so
frugal that she had insisted on taking home her containers

after her McDonald's meal, suddenly handing out twenty dollars for two "children" to splurge on.

"Take it, child," Mrs. Panouvong said. "Now go—you don't want to be late for your test." She smiled. "How nice it'll be when you drive us to work. Think of the time we'll save. And the bus fares."

The money, tucked safely in her coat pocket, seemed to keep Saeng warm on her walk across town to the site of the driving test.

She reached it a few minutes early and stood on the corner, glancing around her. There were a few other teenagers waiting on the sidewalk or sitting on the hoods of their cars, but David was nowhere in sight. On the opposite side of the street was the McDonald's restaurant, and for a moment she imagined how it would be to have David and her sitting at one of the window seats, facing each other, in satisfyingly full view of all the passersby.

A light honk brought her back to reality. David cruised by, waving at her from his car window. He parallel parked the car, with an effortless swerve that Saeng admired, and got out.

"Ready?" David asked, eyebrows arched quizzically as he handed her his car keys.

Saeng nodded. Her mouth suddenly felt dry, and she licked her lips.

"Don't forget: Step on the gas real gently. You don't want to jerk the car forward the way you did last time," David said with a grin.

"I won't," Saeng said, and managed a smile.

Another car drove up, and the test instructor stepped out of it and onto the curb in front of them. He was a pale, overweight man whose thick lips jutted out from behind a bushy mustache. On his paunch was balanced a clipboard, which he was busy marking.

Finally he looked up and saw Saeng. "Miss Saeng Panouvong?" he asked, slurring the name so much that Saeng did not recognize it as her own until she felt David nudge her slightly.

"Y—yes, sir," Saeng answered.

"Your turn. Get in."

Then Saeng was behind the wheel, the paunchy man seated next to her, clipboard on his lap.

"Drive to the end of the street and take a right," the test instructor said. He spoke in a low, bored staccato that Saeng had to strain to understand.

Obediently, she started up the car, careful to step on the accelerator very slowly, and eased the car out into the middle of the street. *Check the rearview mirror, make the hand gestures, take a deep breath,* Saeng told herself.

So far, so good. At the intersection at the end of the street, she slowed down. Two cars were coming down the cross street toward her at quite a high speed. Instinctively, she stopped and waited for them both to drive past. Instead, they both stopped, as if waiting for her to proceed.

Saeng hesitated. Should she go ahead and take the turn before them or wait until they went past?

Better to be cautious, she decided, and waited, switching gears over to neutral.

For what seemed an interminable moment, nobody moved. Then the other cars went through the intersection, one after the other. Carefully, Saeng then took her turn (*turn signal, hand signal, look both ways*).

As she continued to drive down the street, out of the corner of her eye she saw the instructor mark down something on his clipboard.

*A mistake,* she thought. *He's writing down a mistake I just made. But what did I do wrong?* She stole a quick look at his face. It was stern but impassive. *Maybe I should ask him right now, what I did wrong,* Saeng wondered.

"Watch out!" he suddenly exclaimed. "That's a stop sign!"

Startled, Saeng jerked the car to a stop—but not soon enough. They were right in the middle of the crossroads.

The instructor shook his head. An almost imperceptible gesture, but Saeng noted it with a sinking feeling in her stomach.

"Back up," he snapped.

Her heart beating hard, Saeng managed to reverse the car and back up to the stop sign that she had just gone through.

"You might as well go back to where we started out," the instructor said. "Take a right here, and another right at the intersection."

*It's over,* Saeng thought. *He doesn't even want to see me go up the hill or parallel park or anything. I've failed.*

Swallowing hard, she managed to drive the rest of the way back. In the distance she could see the big M archway outside the McDonald's restaurant, and as she approached, she noticed David standing on the opposite curb, hands on his hips, watching their approach.

With gratitude she noticed that he had somehow managed to stake out two parking spaces in a row so that she could have plenty of space to swerve into place.

She breathed a deep sigh of relief when the car was safely parked. Only after she had turned off the ignition did she dare look the instructor in the face.

"How—how did I do, sir?" she asked him, hating the quaver in her own voice.

"You'll get your results in the mail next week," he said in that bored monotone again, as if he had parroted the same sentence countless times. Then he must have seen the anxious, pleading look on Saeng's face, for he seemed to soften somewhat. "You stopped when you didn't need to—you had right of way at that first intersection," he said. "Then at the second intersection, when you should have stopped at the stop sign, you went right through it." He shrugged. "Too bad," he mumbled. Then he was out of the car, clipboard and all, and strolling down the curb to the next car.

It had all happened so quickly. Saeng felt limp. So she had failed. She felt a burning shame sting her cheeks. She had never failed a test before. Not even when she had first arrived in school and had not understood a word they had said, had she ever failed a test.

Tests, always tests—there had been so many tests in the last four years. Math tests, spelling tests, science tests. And for each one she had prepared herself, learned what was expected of her, steeled herself, taken the test, and somehow passed. She thought of the long evenings she had spent at the kitchen table after the dinner dishes had been cleared away, when she and her mother had used their battered English-Lao dictionary to look up virtually every single word in her textbooks and carefully written Lao equivalent above the English word, so that there were faint spidery pencil marks filling up all the spaces between the lines of her textbooks.

All those tests behind her, and now she had failed. Failed the one test that might have enabled her to help her parents get to work more easily, save them some money, and earn her some status among her classmates.

David's face appeared at the window. "How'd it go?" he asked with his usual cheerful grin.

Saeng suppressed an urge to pass her hand over his mouth and wipe the grin off. "Not so good," she said. She started to explain, then gave it up. It wasn't worth the effort, and besides, he didn't really care anyway.

He was holding the car door open for her and seemed a little impatient for her to get out. Saeng squirmed out of the seat, then remembered the twenty-dollar bill her mother had given her.

"Eh . . . thanks," she murmured awkwardly as she got out of the car. "It was nice of you to come here. And letting me use your car."

"Don't mention it," he said, sliding into the driver's seat already and pushing it back several inches.

"Would you . . . I mean, if you'd like, I could buy . . ." Saeng faltered as she saw that David wasn't even listening to her. His attention had been distracted to someone waving to him from across the street. he was waving back and smiling. Saeng followed the direction of his glance and saw a tall girl in tight jeans and a flannel shirt standing just under the M archway. Someone blond and vivacious, her dimpled smile revealing two rows of dazzling, white, regimentally straight teeth. Definitely a cheerleader, Saeng decided.

"Hold on, I'll be right with you," David was calling over to her. Abruptly he pulled the car door shut, flashed Saeng a perfunctory smile, and started to drive off. "Better luck next time," he said as his car pulled away, leaving her standing in the middle of the road.

Saeng watched him make a fluid U-turn and pull up right next to the tall blond girl, who swung herself gracefully into the seat next to David. For a moment they sat there laughing and talking in the car. So carefree, so casual—so American. They reminded Saeng of the Ken and Barbie dolls that she had stared at with such curiosity and longing when she had first arrived in the country.

But it wasn't even longing or envy that she felt now, Saeng realized. This girl could have been David's twin sister, and Saeng would still have felt this stab of pain, this recognition that They Belonged, and she didn't.

Another car drove slowly past her, and she caught a glimpse of her reflection on its window. Her arms were hanging limply by her sides, and she looked short and frumpy. Her hair was disheveled and her clothes seemed drab and old-fashioned—exactly as if they had come out of a rummage sale. She looked wrong. Totally out of place.

"Hey, move it! You're blocking traffic!"

A car had pulled up alongside of her, and in the front passenger seat sat the test instructor scowling at her, his thick lips taut with irritation.

Saeng stood rooted to the spot. She stared at him, stared at those thick lips beneath the bushy mustache. And suddenly she was jolted back to another time, another place, another voice—it had all been so long ago and so far away, yet now she still found herself immobilized by the immediacy of the past.

Once, shortly after she had arrived in America, when she had been watching an absorbing ballet program on the PBS channel at Mrs. Lambert's house, someone had switched channels with a remote control, and it seemed as if the gracefully dying Giselle in Swan Lake had suddenly been riddled with bullets from a screeching getaway car. So jarring had it been that Saeng felt as if an electric shock had charged through her, jolting her from one reality into another.

It was like that now, as if someone had switched channels in her life. She was no longer standing on a quiet street in downtown Danby but in the midst of a jostling crowd of tired, dusty people under a blazing sun. And it was not the balding driving instructor yelling at her, but a thick-lipped man in a khaki uniform, waving at them imperiously with a submachine gun.

Ban Vinai, Thailand. 1978. Things clicked into place, but it was no use knowing the name and number of the channel. The fear and dread still suffused her. She still felt like the scared, bone-weary little girl she had been then, being herded into the barbed-wire fencing of the refugee camp after they had escaped across the Mekong River in Laos.

"What're you doing, standing in the middle of the road? Get out of the way!"

And click—the Thai soldier was the test instructor again. Saeng blinked, blinked away the fear and fatigue of that memory, and slowly that old reality receded. In a daze she turned and made her way over to the curb, stepped up onto it, and started walking away.

*Breathe deep, don't break down,* she told herself fiercely. She could imagine David and that cheerleader staring at her behind her back. *I am tough,* she thought, *I am strong, I can take it.*

The sidewalk was littered with little acorns, and she kicked at them viciously as she walked and walked.

Only when she had turned the corner and was safely out of sight of David and the others did she finally stop. She found herself standing under a huge tree whose widespread branches were now almost leafless. An acorn dropped down and hit her on the head, before bouncing off into the street.

It seemed like the final indignity. Angrily, Saeng reached up for the branch directly overhead and tore off some of the large brown leaves still left. They were dry and crisp as she crushed them in her hands. She threw them at the wind and watched the bits of brown being whipped away by the afternoon wind.

"Who cares about the test, anyway," she said in a tight, grim whisper, tearing up another fistful of oak leaves. "Stupid test, stupid David, stupid cars. Who needs a license, anyway? Who needs a test like that?" It would only get harder, too, she realized, with the winter approaching and the streets turning slippery with the slush and snow. She had barely felt safe walking on the sidewalks in the winter—how could she possibly hope to drive then? It was hopeless, useless to even try. *I won't, I just won't ever take that test again!* Saeng told herself.

That resolved, she felt somewhat better. She turned away from the oak tree and was about to leave, when she suddenly noticed the bush next to it.

There was something very familiar about it. Some of its leaves had already blown off, but those that remained were still green. She picked a leaf and examined it. It was vaguely heart-shaped, with deeply serrated edges. Where had she seen the kind of leaf before? Saeng wondered. And why, among all these foreign maples and oak leaves, did it seem so very familiar? She scrutinized the bush, but it was no help: If there had been any flowers on it, they had already fallen off.

Holding the leaf in her hand, Saeng left the park and started walking home.

Her pace was brisk and determined, and she had not planned to stop off anywhere. But along the way, she found herself pausing involuntarily before a florist shop window. On display were bright bunches of cut flowers in tall glass vases—the splashes of red roses, white carnations, and yellow chrysanthemums a vivid contrast to the gray October afternoon. In the shadows behind them were several potted plants, none of which she could identify.

On an impulse, Saeng swung open the door and entered.

An elderly woman behind the counter looked up and smiled at her. "Yes? Can I help you?" she asked.

Saeng hesitated. Then she thrust out the heart-shaped green leaf in her hand and stammered, "Do—do you have this plant? I—I don't know its name."

The woman took the leaf and studied it with interest. "Why, yes," she said. "That looks like a rose of Sharon. We have several in the nursery out back."

She kept up a steady stream of conversation as she escorted Saeng through a side door into an open courtyard, where various saplings and shrubs stood. "Of course, it's not the best time for planting, but at least the ground hasn't frozen solid yet, and if you dig a deep enough hole and put in some good compost, it should do just fine. Hardy plants, these roses of Sharon. Pretty blossoms, too, in the fall. In fact—look, there's still a flower or two left on this shrub. Nice shade of pink, isn't it?"

Saeng looked at the single blossom left on the shrub. It looked small and washed out. The leaves on the shrub were of the same distinct serrated heart shape, but its flower looked—wrong, somehow.

"Is there—I mean, can it have another kind of flower?" Saeng asked. "Another color, maybe?"

"Well, it also comes in a pale purplish shade," the woman said helpfully. "And white, too."

"I think—I think it was a deep color," she offered, then shook her head. "I don't remember. It doesn't matter." Discouraged and feeling more than a little foolish, she started to back away.

"Wait," the florist said. "I think I know what you're looking for." A slow smile deepened the wrinkles in her face. "Come this way. It's in our greenhouse."

At the far side of the courtyard stood a shed, the like of which Saeng had never seen before. It was made entirely of glass and seemed to be bathed in a soft white light.

As she led the way there, the florist started talking again. "Lucky we just got through moving in some of our tropical plants," she said, "or the frost last weekend would have killed them off. Anything in there now you'd have to leave indoors until next summer, of course. Next to a big south-facing window or under some strong neon lamps. Even so, some of the plants won't survive the long cold winters here. Hothouse flowers, that's what they are. Not hardy, like those roses of Sharon I just showed you."

Only half listening, Saeng wished that there were a polite way she could excuse herself and leave. It was late and she was starting to get hungry. Still, she dutifully followed the other woman through the greenhouse door and walked in.

She gasped.

It was like walking into another world. A hot, moist world exploding with greenery. Huge flat leaves, delicate wisps of tendrils, ferns and fronds and vines of all shades and shapes grew in seemingly random profusion.

"Over there, in the corner, the hibiscus. Is that what you mean?" The florist pointed at a leafy potted plant by the corner.

There, in a shaft of the wan afternoon sunlight, was a single bloodred blossom, its five petals splayed back to reveal a long stamen tipped with yellow pollen. Saeng felt a shock of recognition so intense, it was almost visceral.

"*Saebba*," Saeng whispered.

A *saebba* hedge, tall and lush, had surrounded their garden, its lush green leaves dotted with vermilion flowers. And sometimes after a monsoon rain, a blossom or two would have blown into the well, so that when she drew up the well water, she would find a red blossom floating in the bucket.

Slowly, Saeng walked down the narrow aisle toward the hibiscus. Orchids, lanna bushes, oleanders, elephant ear begonias, and bougainvillea vines surrounded her. Plants that she had not even realized she had known but had forgotten drew her back into her childhood world.

When she got to the hibiscus, she reached out and touched a petal gently. It felt smooth and cool, with a hint of velvet toward the center—just as she had known it would feel.

And beside it was yet another old friend, a small shrub with waxy leaves and dainty flowers with purplish petals and white centers. "Madagascar periwinkle," its tag announced. How strange to see it in a pot, Saeng thought. Back home it just grew wild, jutting out from the cracks in brick walls or between tiled roofs. There had been a patch of it by the little spirit house where she used to help her mother light the incense and candles to the spirit who guarded their home and their family. Sometimes she would casually pick a flower or two to leave on the offerings of fruit and rice left at the altar.

And that rich, sweet scent—that was familiar, too. Saeng scanned the greenery around her and found a tall, gangly plant with exquisite little white blossoms on it. *"Dok Malik,"* she said, savoring the feel of the word on her tongue, even as she silently noted the English name on its tag, "jasmine."

One of the blossoms had fallen off, and carefully Saeng picked it up and smelled it. She closed her eyes and breathed in, deeply. The familiar fragrance filled her lungs, and Saeng could almost feel the light strands of her grandmother's long gray hair, freshly washed, as she combed it out with the fine-toothed buffalo-horn comb. And when the sun had dried it, Saeng would help the gnarled old fingers knot the hair into a bun, then slip a *dok Malik* bud into it.

Saeng looked at the white bud in her hand now, small and fragile. Gently, she closed her palm around it and held it tight. That, at least, she could hold on to. But where was the fine-toothed comb? The hibiscus hedge? The well? Her gentle grandmother?

A wave of loss so deep and strong that it stung Saeng's eyes now swept over her. A blink, a channel switch, a boat ride in the night, and it was all gone. Irretrievably, irrevocably gone.

And in the warm moist shelter of the greenhouse, Saeng broke down and wept.

It was already dusk when Saeng reached home. The wind was blowing harder, tearing off the last remnants of green in the chicory weeds that were growing out of the cracks in the sidewalk. As if oblivious to the cold, her mother was still out in the vegetable garden, digging up the last of the onions with a rusty trowel. She did not see Saeng until the girl had quietly knelt down next to her.

Her smile of welcome warmed Saeng. *"Ghup ma laio le?* You're back?" she said cheerfully. "Goodness, it's past five. What took you so long? How did it go? Did you—?" Then she noticed the potted plant that Saeng was holding, its leaves quivering in the wind.

Mrs. Panouvong uttered a small cry of surprise and delight. *"Dok faeng-noi!"* she said. "Where did you get it?"

"I bought it," Saeng answered, dreading her mother's next question.

"How much?"

For answer Saeng handed her mother some coins.

"That's all?" Mrs. Panouvong said, appalled. "Oh, but I forgot! You and the Lambert boy at Bee-Maags. . . ."

"No, we didn't, Mother," Saeng said.

"Then what else—?"

"Nothing else. I paid over nineteen dollars for it."

"You what?" Her mother stared at her incredulously. "But how could you? All the seeds for this vegetable garden didn't cost that much! You know how much we—" She paused, as she noticed the tearstains on her daughter's cheeks and her puffy eyes.

"What happened?" she asked, more gently.

"I—I failed the test," Saeng said.

For a long moment Mrs. Panouvong said nothing. Saeng did not dare to look at her mother in the eye. Instead, she stared at the hibiscus plant and nervously tore off a leaf, shredding it to bits.

Her mother reached out and brushed the fragments of green off Saeng's hands. "It's a beautiful plant, this *dok faeng-noi*," she finally said. "I'm glad you got it."

"It's—it's not a real one," Saeng mumbled. "I mean, not like the kind we had at—at—." She found that she was still too shaky to say the words at home, lest she burst into tears again. "Not like the kind we had before," she said.

"I know," her mother said quietly. "I've seen this kind blooming along the lake. Its flowers aren't as pretty, but it's strong enough to make it through the cold months here, this winter hibiscus. That's what matters."

She tipped the pot and deftly eased the ball of soil out, balancing the rest of the plant in her other hand. "Look how root-bound it is, poor thing," she said. "Let's plant it, right now."

She went over to the corner of the vegetable patch and started to dig a hole in the ground. The soil was cold and hard, and she had trouble thrusting the shovel into it. Wisps of her gray hair trailed out in the breeze, and her slight frown deepened the wrinkles around her eyes. There was a frail, wiry beauty to her that touched Saeng deeply.

"Here, let me help, Mother," she offered, getting up and taking the shovel away from her.

Mrs. Panouvong made no resistance. "I'll bring in the hot peppers and bitter melons, then, and start dinner. How would you like an omelet with slices of the bitter melon?"

"I'd love it," Saeng said.

Left alone in the garden, Saeng dug out a hole and carefully lowered the "winter hibiscus" into it. She could hear the sounds of cooking from the kitchen now, the beating of the eggs against the bowl, the sizzle of hot oil in the pan. The pungent smell of bitter melon wafted out, and Saeng's mouth watered. It was a cultivated taste, she had discovered—none of her classmates or friends, not even Mrs. Lambert, liked it—this sharp, bitter melon that left a golden aftertaste on the tongue. But she had grown up eating it and, she admitted to herself, much preferred it to a Big Mac.

The "winter hibiscus" was in the ground now, and Saeng tamped down the soil around it. Overhead, a flock of Canada geese flew by, their faint honks clear and—yes—familiar to Saeng now. Almost reluctantly, she realized that many of the things that she had thought of as strange before had become, through the quiet repetition of season upon season, almost familiar to her now. Like the geese. She lifted her head and watched as their distinctive V was etched against the evening sky, slowly fading into the distance.

*When they come back,* Saeng vowed silently to herself, *in the spring, when the snows melt and the geese return and this hibiscus is budding, then I will take that test again.*

■ ■ ■

# Pam Muñoz Ryan

Pam Muñoz Ryan was born and raised in California's San Joaquin Valley. Her grandparents on her mother's side came to the U.S. from Mexico in the 1930s, but her heritage is also part Spanish, Basque, Italian and Oklahoman.

After college Ryan became a teacher, then a friend encouraged her to start writing. She is now a full-time writer and the author of ten books for children and young adults, including *Riding Freedom, Esperanza Rising, California Here We Come!* and *The Flag We Love.*

Pam Muñoz Ryan lives in Leucadia, California with her husband and four children.

■ ■ ■